EDUCATION, GANDHI AND MAN

EDUCATION, GANDHI AND MAN

Select Writings

Khwaja Ghulamus Saiyyadain

Edited by

Akhtarul Wasey

Farhat Ehsas

SHIPRA

Rs. 160; US$ 8

ISBN: 978-81-7541-388-7

2014 Impression
(2008)

Education, Gandhi and Man

Published by:
SHIPRA PUBLICATIONS
H.O.: LG 18-19, Pankaj Central Market, I.P. Ext.,
Patparganj, Delhi 110092, Ph. 22235152, 22236152
Br. Off.: 4617/18, Main Ansari Road, Daryaganj,
New Delhi 110002; Ph.9650028065, 9810522367
Email: info@shiprapublications.com
Website: www.shiprapublications.com

To
Saiyyada Aapa who not only inherited
but kept alive the intellectual fervor of
Saiyyedain Saheb.

Preface

Much has changed since the days when **Khwaja Ghulamus Saiyyadain** lived, thought and worked. It was a time when many of the good old values of our traditional social and cultural life were still living and had a vigorous presence in our day-to-day life. Age-old neighbourhoods in villages, small towns, even in big cities, were intact with all their intimacies of relationship, interactions and togetherness. People knew each other at close quarters. Urbanisation was yet to take off with the pace it took after independence. The idea and image of an educated, cultured gentleman/gentlewoman still had its value and meaning because there were a lot of people who exemplified this idea and image. The defining features of that social and cultural environment were a sense of purpose and fulfillment in life, commitment to values, trustworthiness, dependability and credibility, firmness of views and steadfastness in behaviour and action. It was this commitment to values that made people trust each other and also make sacrifices. There was also a sense of collective interests, commitment to public or societal causes that informed a good Indian's priorities in life and personal interests more often than not were sacrificed to valiantly serve the collective interests.

Intellectual discourse was also not as complex and contorted as it gradually became. There was an astonishing simplicity informing every field of knowledge where the subject and the object of knowledge were always bound in a communion. Seeking of knowledge was a mission, and not a profession. Educational institutions were to a large extent, at least in the their commitment to ideals, were wedded to this holistic and socially committed view of knowledge and education. Teachers commanded a respect that was a voluntary response from the students, and not out of the fear that today keeps students under perpetual threat.

Khwaja Sahab was indeed a traditional man but in a more rewarding sense of the term. He inherited all the good values of the social, cultural and religious ethos that the Indo-Islamic civilization offered to a sensitive and intelligent human being. But he did not remain confined to these illuminating effects of the tradition but used them to further enlighten his mental horizons whereas he enriched his mind with modern knowledge.

But beyond all the cultural refinements and intellectual achievements that Khwaja Sahb was able to attain, what makes him stand out was his firm belief in the universal values of Islam and his equally strong belief in the commonness and inner compatibilities between core Islamic and Indian civilizational values. All his life he tried with all his powers of mind and heart to preach and promote the values of tolerance and peaceful co-existence that he thought and believed were two foundations on which can rest the edifice of a modern India that includes all and excludes none.

The articles that form the basis and reason of this book contain in abundance the brilliant wit, erudition and commitment to values that have been the defining features of Khwaja Ghulamus Saiyyadain's genius and his mission.

I believe that the book will be able to rekindle some of the flames of the moral and intellectual brilliance that our not so distant past radiated, illumining our ways of thought and action amidst the present darkness.

Akhtarul Wasey

Acknowledgement

I am grateful to Dr. Saiyyada Saiyyedain Hamid, Member, Planning Commission and a noted literary figure for helping us in identifying some of the writings included in this publication.

I am also thankful to my colleague Mr. Farhat Ehsas without whom I have not been able to engage myself in bringing out many scholarly publications like this. I must thank my other colleagues at the Zakir Husain Institute of Islamic studies, Jamia Millia Islamia, particularly Mr. Ataur Rehman and Mr. Mohd. Nasim Haider for the help and cooperation which was received from them. Last but not the least, I thank Mr. D. Kumar of the Shipra publications for this publication.

Prof. Akhtarul Wasey

Contents

1

New Challenges to Education

It is with a feeling of keen poignancy that I have accepted the honour of delivering this first Jha Memorial Lecture at the invitation of the All-India Federation of Educational Associations. It is a great pity that this veteran educationist should have been so suddenly snatched away from us, when his cultured counsels of wisdom were needed so urgently in our developing and difficult educational situation. I had the privilege of knowing him over a long period of years—ever since my student days in fact and had developed both admiration and affection for him. He had some of the finest qualities—I shall refer to three of them—that are needed in a true educationist. He was essentially a man of culture—culture based not only on the humanistic studies but also on humanism and, as you can well appreciate the two do not always or even frequently go together. I have known persons—who has not?—who have made a scholarly study of literature or art or philosophy or other disciplines but whose hearts and minds have remained essentially uncultivated and uncultured. They have found a place in their memory but not illumined their minds and left their hearts cold and untouched. Jha, on the other hand, had a mind that was quickened by his scholarship and a heart that was warmed and enriched by the great ideas and noble emotions which confer immortality on classics. I presume it was this quality, coupled with his sensitive love of books and all that they stand for in life, which made him a much loved and admired teacher for decades. He had a great catholicity of interests which is also an important hall-mark of true culture. To give but one instance he was a great advocate of Hindi but, even in the days of acute Urdu-Hindi controversy, his appreciation of the richness and significance of Urdu language and literature remained unimpaired and he extended his generous friendship and patronage to Urdu writers and poets with the same readiness as to writers of Hindi. Again, he had great courage of his intellectual and professional convictions and was not afraid to espouse views and causes which happened to be unpopular. In a world, which is dominated by conformity and where the teacher even when he rises to eminence, is apt to be rather timid and apologetic in the expression of his views, it is heartening to find some one who had the intellectual integrity to differ from popular or authoritative trends of opinion. I did not always agree with his views but always respected them for their frankness and vigour. A third quality in him which specially endeared him to the teaching profession was his fearless and forthright advocacy of the need for improving the teachers material prospects. There are many public men and others who keep on reminding them of their duties and responsibilities but he was specially sensitive to the other side of the picture—namely, that it was not possible for them to discharge these duties worthily and efficiently, even with the best will in the world, if they were unable to meet their bare material needs...deeper Culture in its sense, which includes but transcends scholarship, intellectual integrity and respect for the teaching profession—these are qualities which need to be specially stressed in this country both for teachers and non-teachers and, in paying our tribute today to the memory of Dr. Amaranatha Jha, we would do well to forge or strengthen our links with them.

Why are these and many other cognate qualities of special significance in our present context? Taking advantage of the opportunity provided by this platform. I might venture to share a few of my strong convictions and ideas with you in regard to the nature of the challenge which education faces today in India. This challenge seems not only from the basic objectives and purposes which underlie the educative process but also derives its special colour and texture from the total objective situation that exists in the country. I have sometimes the anxious feeling that many of us, who are engaged in the task of teaching or guiding educational policies and programmes, are either unaware of the urgency and implications of the challenge or our awareness is only superficial—something that finds expression occasionally in speeches and writings but does not mould our pattern of work from day to day. If the inspiration of really creative and humanisitc tradition does not permeate our educational activities vigorously, there is a serious danger that a good deal of what is being done in the way of national reconstruction may collapse like a wall of sand without foundations. If we analyse the human situation carefully, we cannot escape the conclusion that there is no way to preserve all that is good or great in our culture and civilization—or to add to it—except through improvements in the basic quality and efficiency of the human personality. All social, political and economic reconstruction involves many difficult and complicated problems and, with almost every day that passes, these complications are becoming more intense. On the social and political side, the tremendously increased intercourse between groups and nations has multiplied a hundred—or, who knows, a thousand—fold the ramifications of our actions and programme. On the economic side, science and industrialization and the rapid growth of populations have given not only a new dimension to our problems but in some ways altered their basic nature. Anything that we do, in one part of the world has not only its repercussions in other remote parts but they express themselves in unsuspected ways which our great advances in knowledge are still unable to anticipate! In spite of these difficulties, however, and without being deterred by them we have launched upon many gigantic projects—of dam reconstruction, industrialization, of nationalized business enterprises, of reclamation of land, of improved agriculture, of health services and housing—which are being gradually put under way. It is possible through forced marches, as it were, and with the help of emergency measures—like foreign aid, foreign technicians and our own technicians trained in a hurry—to carry these schemes to completion. But that is at best only a short-lived victory or achievement, unless we can side by side take imaginative and long-term measures to train up gradually the kind of human personnel that will be able to stand up to the intellectual as well as the technical strain of the burden that it will have to carry. In one sense, it is an obvious fact—a River Valley project or a National Laboratory will not function unless trained engineers and scientists are available in the market and are utilized to keep them running. But this is true in a deeper and wider sense also where it is not merely a matter of the demand and supply of technical personnel on certain feasible terms but of planning beforehand for the regular and steady flow of young scientists, engineers, social scientist, doctors, scholars and other qualified persons who will keep the caravan moving through the years. It is important to remember, however, that this is not just a problem to technical training in the rather specific sense of producing people who possess the requisite know-how of the processes and skills involved. One can with a touch of fantasy, imagine robots who may be able to carry on many of these processes which science can reduce to purely mechanical terms with increasing range and efficiency. But robots can never take the place of human beings, who can think and feel and act with a considerable degree of freedom. The task of education, therefore, is not merely that of turning out first-rate technicians and scientists but, even more urgently and basically it is the task of training good men and women, with a quality of goodness which includes both technical efficiency and human efficiency in its broadest sense. An engineer or scientist or doctor who can manipulate his machines or apparatus and conduct his experiments successfully but is unable to understand and sympathize with his fellow worker and his fellow men, whose mind is not quickened to the magic of ideas and responsive to decent emotions—such a person is, in the last analysis, a poor technician and a poor human being. In planning their education, therefore, we have to plan imaginatively and from the earliest stages of educations so that the structure of character and personality may be built up, brick by brick from the very beginning. I shall return presently to what I regard as the right shape and components of this structure.

Let us revert for a moment to the problem of analysing the main features of our objective situation. The country is faced not only with the problem of fighting poverty and unemployment and providing people with food, houses, clothing, transport and other essential facilities for a reasonably comfortable life. These are very important as a starting point but as a starting point only. The full life or the "abundant life" as Jesus Christ called it, has to be nourished not only on the food for the body but also food for the spirit and it must provide certain conditions which are necessary for both, such as health, physical as well as mental freedom without which integrity, thought and action are alike impossible and release from the bondage of fear and superstition which thwart man at every turn. We have, therefore, to envisage the situation in civic and political terms also and ask ourselves: What are the essential requirements of the secular democratic socialistic State which we are aspiring to set up? What are the qualities needed in such a set-up and how can they be translated into pedagogical and curricular terms?

It is not that these questions are frightfully hard to answer. What is difficult is to believe in them with such intensity that they become the inspiration and motive force of our individual and collective conduct and on the pedagogical side to project them into all that goes on in our schools and colleges day after day, hour by hour. No great argument is needed to persuade persons of average intelligence and decency that certain qualities are essential ingredients in the character of a creative citizen who is well integrated in such a social order. He must be able to share actively in the common weal and woe and share common burdens willingly and not play for his lone hand. Narrowness of outlook and loyalties, attachment to selfish interest are out of tune with democratic citizenship. Secondly, he should have a reasonable modicum of capacity to think for himself and understand the outstanding problems of contemporary world about which, as a citizen, he is expected to express his opinions and give his vote. An ignorant, credulous and gullible electrorate is a happy hunting ground for the unscrupulous demagogue but not an asset to democracy! Thirdly, he should honour all useful and productive work, should be ready to participate in it willingly and, in doing so, take pride in efficiency and good craftsmanship, whatever the work entrusted to him. This also provides the ultimate justification for the great stress that is placed on discipline—without discipline, no worthwhile work can be done. A nation of inefficient or indisciplined and ease-loving parasites—or where such a type is tolerated complacently—can never achieve its full stature or make its best contribution to the world, for in life, there may be alternatives to almost everything but there is no alternative to good, honest work. In the fourth place, we have to ensure the rule of social justice in our collective life and that postulates the cultivation of social sensitiveness, of charity and compassion, in the ethical sense, towards sections and classes which are underprivileged and the adoption of measures which will give institutional forms to this feeling. In addition to these qualities which are equally necessary in every democracy, we have also to recognize that our country is essentially a land of variety—variety of races, religions, languages and cultures which from the warp and woof from which the fabric of its richness has been woven. It is, therefore, a condition both of its survival and its greatness that we should appreciate this variety and make it not an excuse for internecine conflicts and quarrels but a reason for developing tolerance, understanding and the art of living together gracefully with those who differ from us. Democracy will fall like a house of cards if we do not learn this art quickly and sincerely but allow the present dissensions and fanaticisms to embitter our relations. The recent experience in this field are a sharp warning that we can ignore only at our peril. And that applies to international level where the variety is even greater and the only alternative to living together amicable is the dubious satisfaction of collective annihilation.

I started with saying that education was faced with a peculiarly urgent challenge and I have tried to analyse somewhat sketchily the nature of this challenge in human terms. If you ponder over them, you will notice that luckily the demands the objective situation makes are in harmony with the basic objectives and purposes which educationists of vision have always cherished and advocated—practical efficiency and high technical skill, appreciation of the dignity of work, clarity of mind, community of interests, purposes and loyalties with our fellow citizens, compassion and tolerance. If our education does not do anything or enough, to inculcate these qualities, it has failed grievously to meet the challenge that it faces, This is precisely the problem of educational reorganization with which we are all concerned in our different ways and, though its ultimate purposes may be obscured in our preoccupations with specific details, a true educationist should never lose sight of them, for it is only then that he can steer his course with faith and a sense of direction. The change in methods and curricula and techniques of discipline that is advocated at the stage of basic education the broadbasing and activizing of Secondary Education, the emphasis on genuine mental training and research in the Universities and the importance of developing social activities and free social relationships at all levels derive their ultimate justification from precisely the same source and the desire to help in the emergence of a type of educated person who will be able to play his part worthily in the new world that is gradually emerging but will never emerge fully and clearly unless he takes a hand intelligently in shaping it.

The rationalizing of the educational pattern is one of the first steps that we have had to take in this connection and its landmarks are now fairly clear. We want to develop a system of mass education which will cover seven to eight years and during which children will not only acquire the basic minimum skill in the three tool subjects but also a broad elementary understanding of their world and the habits and attitudes which make for decent, co-operative and disciplined living. The emphasis would be not on scholastic achievement or burdening the memory with useless knowledge but with quickening their interests and releasing their creative impulses in an atmosphere of freedom and community living. This should be followed by four years of Secondary Education which will be more broadbased and practical than the traditional pattern, which will explore and stimulate their varied aptitudes more consciously, where the emphasis will shift on active acquisition of knowledge and training in co-operative life. The endeavour would be to raise standards high enough to enable the student to enter into a vocation or a profession or to find a place in the University with requisite intellectual competence. Cutting out the unnecessary and wasteful hurdle of an Intermediate Examination, the three-year degree course will equip the University students with the capacity for clear thinking and clear expression, with interest not only in their particular subjects but in all the broad areas of human knowledge and artistic appreciation and above all, a balanced and humanized outlook which might provide a bulwark against the prejudices and fanaticism of various kinds which flourish unchecked in many groups an regions. To advocate such a system all over the country or to stress these aims is not to impose any rigid uniformity—as some people have wrongly alleged—but to ensure that the future of the country is not mortgaged to perverted ideologies or anti-social and fissiparous tendencies.

Within this broad framework, we should pour all the creativity, the originality, the vision and the devotion of which we are capable, refusing to be content with instructional efficiency which enables students to pass examinations. As we carry on our teaching assignments from day to day teaching lessons, correcting exercises, supervising projects and experimental work, organizing games and social activities, we should be constantly asking ourselves many basic questions and taking the risk of giving honest replies: "Are we quickening our students' minds? Are we developing their critical capacities which will turn mercilessly upon themselves but sympathetically on others? Are we enlarging their sympathies and deepening their human understanding so that they will not think and feel and act in the narrow and dark grooves of class and creed and caste loyalties but in the day-light of national and human interests? Are we teaching them to be honest and courageous and free in their everyday dealings or implanting unlovely complexes for which they will have to suffer and pay in the long run? Can they distinguish between the beautiful and the ugly or does their education leave them aesthetically blind? Have they cultivated the humble decencies of civic life which make for harmony and cleanliness and pleasant social relations or do they continue to act in uncouth and boorish ways when they are given their head?" I dare not say that these things are easy to achieve but I am firmly convinced that they are the only things really worth striving for. They alone provide the touchstone on which you can test the genuineness of the coin that you are passing on to them. Perhaps you will permit me to share with you what I said a few years ago to a Conference of Bombay Head Masters whom I had advised to take their colleagues into confidence and to make education into a co-operative adventure of significance.

"Friends, we are engaged in doing educational work at a very critical period in the history of our country and the history of the world. It is, no doubt, beset with great difficulties—including the economic difficulties and handicaps under which we have to labour—but is also a great adventure: an adventure of the spirit, fraught with infinite possibilities. Our country, harassed by many obstinate and heart-rending problems and our world, obsessed with misery and war and destruction and the menace of Atom Bomb, have no protection against these dangers and no hope against the onslaught of the forces of evil except what we can do through education in its widest sense—through our own feeble but sincere efforts, with our weak but unwavering hands—to restore the world to sanity and reason and the joy of creative, peaceful work. This battle has to be fought in every home and every school and within the heart and soul of every growing child and youth. It has to be fought against the Devil who sits at his counter buying human souls with his dirty but unlimited coins—coins of fear and greed and prejudice and the just for power and the love of pleasure. We must strive to make these coins appear worthless in the eyes of our children so that when they grow up they will be able to distinguish between gold and tinsel, so that, when the testing time comes, their values will be right: they will have learnt to prefer co-operative effort to self-seeking competition, and joy of creative work to possessive happiness, the quality of charity to domination, the virtue of tolerance to fanaticism."

2

The Relevance of Gandhi to Social Reconstruction with Special Reference to Education

To understand the work of any person in its fullness, it is necessary to have some idea of him as a man. While this is generally true, it applied with special force to a man like Gandhi whose life and work were an unbroken continuity, each illumined by the other. My purpose in this paper is a survey of neither but only to present a brief, and, I am afraid, rather inadequate view of one of its manifold facets, that is Gandhi's relevance for social reconstruction in our time with special reference to the role of Education. However, it is necessary to stress to points by way of preamble. Gandhi was at once what his critics would call a starry-eyed idealist and a stern, business like realist. In choosing his values and ideals and goals he was unapologetically idealistic; in the selection of his techniques and methods a realist. As my friend, Shri Ramachandran once put it, *he was an unbelievable amalgam of rose petal and cast steel.* Rose petals when he was dealing with fellow men and women, cast steel when it was a matter of his basic principles—of truth, in particular, as he saw it. You could always disagree with him but you could not in fairness doubt his sincerity. He had an uncompromising integrity of intellect and character. People often say and write things because they sound right but in real life keep at a comfort distance from their platform rhetoric. Not so Gandhi. He not only meant all that he said and wrote but for him a thought in the morning was a deed by nightfall, so far as it was humanly possible. He had his faith, his convictions even his fads but they were, part of him and he was prepared to pay the price for what he held to be right, unmindful alike of public acclaim or public censure. As I said, his life was a unity, not a patchwork of unrelated fragments, all its parts fitting neatly into one another.

He wanted education to be moulded into a certain pattern because he was convinced that, without it, the good life as he saw it, could not come into being. And neither this good life nor good education was possible except in the context of what he considered a good social order in which decent man and women could live fruitfully. So he envisaged, education to use his own words as 'the spearhead of a social revolution' which would enable life to move forward towards peace, justice and cooperation. He was not interested in it only because it trained people to earn their living or because it could be a means of self-expression or a tool for accumulating wealth or power or even the graces of culture. He was deeply involved mentally and emotionally, in the whole panorama of human life—its greatness and triumphs as well as its tragedies, its meanness, and deprivations. He was dedicated to the promotion of the former and the eradication or the reduction of the latter. In fact, if I may say so, his focus of immediate interest was even more—the elimination of the miseries and injustices which dogged the life of the majority of mankind. Life could not raise to its destined greatness, unless the decks were cleared for action by removing all that cramped and crippled it—poverty, ignorance, disease, superstition, intolerance. In this crusade for the good life, he wanted to enlist the service of education. The interest in education, which had been with him most of his life, developed significantly and became a part of his over-all national programme in the last decade of his life. Not as a result of any theoretical or academic study but as a result of his work and experience amongst the masses in the social, political, and economic field. He came to realize vividly that, while some important problems might be dealt with on an urgent, ad-hoc basis, no fundamental revolution in national thinking and behaviour could be brought about without utilizing a radically reorganized education to give a new outlook and ideology to the youth of the country. Otherwise, they will go on repeating the follies and mistakes of the older generation or be moved by the force of counter suggestion neither of which can't by itself provide right guidance.

Education in India, as Gandhi saw, as may of us had seen, was completely out of touch both with the realities of national life and the upsurge of national aspirations. It was not related to the new forces that were stirring in the world; it gave youth little insight in their national culture, neither it strengths not it weaknesses. The preservation of the *status quo* was not only in the interest of the foreign Government but also of the local vested interests, social and economic which controlled whatever influence, power and money were available to the Indians. Gandhi challenged the teachers and educational authorities to look at education with fresh, unclouded eyes and face some fundamental questions. Why are you running this educational system—just because it is usual for every civilized country to do so, or because without it you cannot keep things as they are, or because you are committed to the ideal of building up of a new man in a new world? With the first two alternatives, he was not concerned; it was the last which claimed he loyalty. Education could not be revolutionized, unless it defined its objectives clearly. He said: 'By education I mean an all round drawing out of the best in child and man-body, mind and spirit. Literacy is not the end of education nor even its beginning. It is only one of the means whereby man and woman can be educated, literacy in itself is no education. I would, therefore, begin the child's education by teaching it a useful handicraft and enabling it to produce from the moment it begins it training. A proper and all round development of the mind can take place only when it proceeds *pari passu* with the education of the physical and spiritual faculties of the child. They constitute an indivisible whole.... The utterly false idea the intelligence can be developed only through book reading should give place of the truth that the quickest development of the mind can be achieved by artisan's work being learnt in a scientific manner.... Literary training by itself adds not an inch to one's moral height and character building is independent of literary training.' (This is not a continuous quotation from Gandhi but I have put several small quotations together to bring out some of his basic educational ideas.)

What are the important implications of this statement? Gandhi did not believe that the attainment of literacy was identical with or even closely related to education in the deeper and wider sense. To him the training of the mind was not enough; it was necessary to educate emotions and the powers of the spirit also and this could not be done effectively unless the whole education process was carried on as an integral, indivisible whole. Intelligence can only grow as it come into contact with practical problems and is used to solve them. The book can facilitate the process; book learning cannot take it place. At the centre of the educative process should be work—work with the hands aided by the mind, work which is productive and socially useful, work in which the child (or the adult) can find personal satisfaction and an expression of his budding powers and which help to relate the individual significantly to the country of bridge the gulf between them. Gandhi derived his insight into these great values of work by actually working among the people, by seeing how they worked and learnt and how work influenced their personality and development. He was not primarily concerned with problems of curriculum or methods of teaching, on which he did not claim to be an authority, but attacked the heart of the problem which was to orient education to the real needs and psychology of the people particularly those living in rural areas and representing 80% of the total population. He saw that their life did *not* turn round theoretical or academic knowledge but round practical activities. If school education was not related to them and children were expected only to assimilate knowledge painfully, at second or third hand, without understanding its relevance to their life, it could not possibly quicken their minds or stimulate their creativity. Such work however, was important to home not merely because it was to occupy the centre of the stage in their life but there were a number of other reasons, all strengthening his central thesis. One cannot acquire knowledge effectively and retain it firmly unless it is the result of participation in appropriate social activities. They will on the one hand, challenge one's interest, one's curiosity, one's sense of adventure, one's desire to make and break things and, on the other being learners face of face with problems which require new knowledge for their solution. Learning in such a context is likely to become highly motivated and an integral part of one's personality, instead of being merely a burden on the memory. This may be described and the intellectual justification of learning through doing about which there is considerable agreement among educators. Gandhi did not rate very highly knowledge which failed to irradiate life, which remained 'elitist.' There was also in his view a significant *social* justification for work with the hands. He wanted *all* children rich or poor, high caste or low caste, to join in it so that they may learn the dignity of labour at first hand a social imperative in this country which perhaps other people may not fully appreciate. For him, work did *not* mean just doing anything, without a social purpose; it was an attempt to initiate every child into the significant activities and occupations of community life, so that it may create a sense of identification between the individual and the community. He would have endorsed Carlyle's high definition of work: 'All true work is blessed; he that hath this blessedness let him ask for no other.' Dr. Zakir Hussain who gave educational shape to his broad ideas, underlined its great significance in one of his addresses in these noble words which I have translated from Urdu; 'All work is not educative. It is educative only when it is preceded by mental effort, when it serves some value higher then our selfish ends to which we are devoted. He who works for his own ends may become *skilled;* he does not become *educated.* In the service of values, man does not seek his own enjoyment but strives to achieve perfection in his work, to improve his character and to become a real human being.... Let those who wish to make work the medium of education remember that work is *not* purposeless; that it is not content with any results that may follow. Work does *not* mean the passing of time by doing any haphazard things; it is *not* amusement; it is *not* play; it is *work;* it is purposeful striving. Work sits in judgement on itself with the strictness of an enemy, and, when it passes the test it yields joy unparalleled and unsurpassed. Work is worship' Gandhi always worked in this spirit and his high ambition was that something of this spirit may pass into his fellow men and women so that society may be enriched by the value which flow from such work.

Formal education, as given in India and most other countries in the world, has become quite cut off from the joy, the thrill and the sense of reality which characterize true work. This is so not only in big urban centres, where the sophistication of modern civilization has tended to make many things artificial, but even in rural areas where children generally live closer to nature, except when they go to prison houses called schools! Educational reform in many countries has tried with but limited success, to bridge this gulf the adopting special measures and bringing the children nearer to earth. We have to realize that, like the giant Antaeus man can gain his full strength only when his feet are firmly and literally planted on earth. I have often asked myself—and I have no doubt Gandhi must have asked himself too—how exactly this restoring of education to its earlier vigour and realism can be brought about in big cosmopolitan centres like Tokyo, New York, London and Calcutta, where most people live in high-rise buildings several storeys removed from the earth, where neither educative manual work, nor trees, grass and flowers nor the magic of the changing season enter as vital factors in their every day life. Yet it is necessary to ask bold question and look for imaginative replies. It would be cowardice and lack of wisdom to concentrate on the noisiest problems and forget the most important ones because they appear to be or are difficult. Gandhi did both—particularly raise bold questions. To a generation, which appeared to have reconciled itself to drifting helplessly with the rushing currents of the times, he posed the challenge: Must was accept tamely and unquestioningly the rigidities, the crudities, the injustice of our industrial and capitalistic or totalitarian civilization? Or can we break through their strangle hold and try to build something more humane, more gracious, more equitable, more likely to permit man's infinite potentialities to blossom? In a couplet one of our great poets, Iqbal, refers to a conversation between God and man:

Good asked me: Is this world of mine congenital to thee?
I said 'No' and he answered: 'Then shatter it to bits'

Gandhi was not afraid to take on this (if you like) magnificently impossible challenge. For him, the precious soul of man was the most important thing in the Universe and he was always prepared, like the fabulous American lawyer, Daniel Webster, to wrestle for it with the Devil himself! But is this task really impossible? If with the help of scientific and technological knowledge and expertise a massive cooperative endeavour, man can go to the moon, why with the necessary vision and determination, can he not also solve his social and economic problems on earth? He did not ask for the conquest of the Moon but for the conquest of *man*. He wanted, through the reordering of man's social and economic environment and institutions and through education, to change his motivation, he desires his ambition and attitudes. He recognized that material things were important upto a certain point—to the point where they are used to meet the genuine needs of hundreds of millions of persons living below the subsistence level. In other words, they are important so long as they help to remove hunger and poverty and disease and give man an opportunity to us the powers of his mind and spirit freely. But not otherwise.

Let me not give the impression that Gandhi was opposed in principle to the application of science and technology to human life. It is true that some time the force and uncompromising integrity with which he expressed his opinions gave this impression. But a careful study of his writings makes it clear that he questioned not the *use* of machinery but the *purpose* for which it was used. How and why, he asked, is it being used? I will let him speak for himself:

'What I object to is the craze for machinery, not machinery as such. The craze is for what they call labour-saving machinery. Men go on saving labour till thousands are without work to be thrown on the open streets to die of starvation. I want to save time and labour *not* for a fraction of mankind but for *all*. I want the concentration of wealth not in the hands of a few but in the hands of all. Today machinery merely helps a few to ride on the back of millions. The impetus behind it is to the philosophy to save labour but greed. It is against the constitution of things that I am fighting with all my might. I would favour the use of the most elaborate machinery, if thereby India's pauperism and resulting idleness (could) be avoided. Industrial-isation on a mass scale will necessarily lead to passive or active exploitation of the villagers, and the problems of competition and marketing come in.'

In Gandhiji's scheme of social reconstruction, there was no room for the unceasing multiplication of goods, their demand whetted by powerful media of mass propaganda, over which billions of dollars were being spent all over the world. These recourses could be spent more usefully and reasonably to improve the standard of people living below the barest level of subsistence. When the production of goods becomes the main inspiration of people's life and work, when all scientific and technological expertise is exploited to add to the power and wealth of a comparatively small section of the population unmindful of the general social good, it must be stoutly resisted.

This plethora of goods, not only obscures the joys of the simple life but is also the harbinger of the rivalry, the cut-throat competition, the accentuation of differences between the rich and the poor, the wars between nations and conflicts between groups with no holds barred which bedevil modern society and for which Gandhi found no justification. He had no use for the 'civilized' but lawless jungle in which an increasing number of people had elected or were forced to live. He raised his clear voice of protest against it, unmindful of the risk that he may be called a reactionary, setting back the hands of the clock of time. He wanted a society based on non-violence, on peace, on justice, on freedom of the individual within reason and on the principles of cooperation. The increasing materialization and commercial-ization of modern life and culture was a source of deep anxiety to him, everyone trying to live up to his more affluent next door neighbour! He worked for a society in which man, every man, the least important man would be considered more important than either Pharoah's wealth or the power of the greatest empire or the technological triumphs of the 20th century. He would have organized the life of the country and the nation on that basis but you will find it very difficult to describe himself in the usual political terms like the capitalist or socialist or communist. Nor could an orthodox adherent of any of these creeds probably accept him as belonging to his party. This thinking and personality overflowed these categories; he could not be contained within their rigidly defined frontiers. Perhaps he could only be defined as a humanist who accepted whatever he considered to be good from all sources and the test of goodness for him: Does it raise the quality of life, knock down walls of separateness between man and man and deepen compassion? He did ask, for example, that the doors of the temples be thrown open to the Harijans but that was, for him, a symbolic gesture what he was, in fact, pleading for was the throwing open of the temple of our hearts to the deprived, the under privileged and the exploited. He did not ask the people to divest themselves of unnecessary and dispensable goods but he insisted even more that the habits and attitudes which made them value goods more than human beings be eradicated—greed, envy, fanaticism, lust for power, desire to exploit others for one's own benefit. He stood valiantly for social and political freedom but he had no use of freedom which was used only to fatten one's ego and failed to accept it necessary obligations of freedom. If *apparent* freedom meant, really meant neglecting the good of all, he would have none of it. Thus would have failed to see the logic of a free society which would spend millions of dollars on cancer research leading to the conclusion that smoking was favourable to the development of certain types of cancer and then spend millions more on aggressively advertising cigarettes ! And to cover up this Pickwickian but tragic anamoly the brilliant suggestion has been mooted that every packet of cigarettes should bear the legend that smoking is a great damage to health ! This kind of freedom for all degenerates into a 'free for all' with no place for any over-arching ethic. Such an approach which blurs the distinction between what is good and bad, right and wrong could have no place of Gandhi's Scheme of things.

Gandhi was no narrow minded fanatic wedded to a narrow concept of life or culture. His deep humanism, his charity, his compassion made it impossible for him to be narrow in heart of mind. He has said: 'Cleanse your heart of all narrowness and make it as broad as the Ocean. That is the teaching of the Quran and the Gita.'

In the foyer of the Broadcasting House of Delhi in inscribed this revealing quotation from him 'I do not want my house to be walled in on all sides or my windows to be stuffed. I want the culture of all lands to be blown about my house as freely as possible. Mine is not the religion of the prison house. He wanted this idea to become the inspiration of all our social, educational and cultural endeavours—in fact, to find acceptance all over the world: 'The Indian culture of our times (he stated) is in the making. Many of us are striving to produce a blend of all the cultures which seem today to be in clash with one another. No culture can live if it attempts to be exclusive. There is no such thing as pure Aryan culture in existence in India. Our new culture stands for the synthesis of the different cultures that have come to stay in India that have influenced Indian life and that in their turn have been influenced by the spirit of the soil.'

At the same time he clearly realized the nature of the relationship between culture and work. Culture grew out of *work* done with integrity and with stress on excellence. He also knew that culture meant very little for persons who could not afford even one full meal a day. There was once an interesting public debate between him and Tagore on this subject. The poet has written in his inimitably lyrical style of how man could derive great joy and satisfaction from the beauties of art and nature, the glorious dawn, the colourful dusk, the magical procession of seasons, the freshness of trees and flowers, the creation of painting and music. Gandhi gently joined issue with him.

'True to his poetical instinct the poet lives for the morrow and would have us do likewise. He presents to our admiring gaze the beautiful pictures of the birds early in the morning, singing hymns of praise as they soar into the sky. These birds have had their day's food and soared with rested wings, in whose veins new blood had flown during the previous night. But I have had the pain of watching birds, who for want of strength, could not be coaxed even into a flutter of their wings. The human bird under the Indian sky gets up weaker than when he pretended to retire.... It is an indescribably painful state which has got to be experienced to be realized. I have found it impossible to soothe suffering patients which a song from Kabir. The hungry millions ask for one poem—

invigorating food. They cannot be given it. They must earn it. And they can earn only by the sweat of their brow.'

This meant, in effect: 'Do not talk about culture till you have at least made sure that people have the necessary material infrastructure for it'—a significant statement when made by a man like Gandhi who had the most lively appreciation of the riches of the spirit! So keen, so poignant was his realization of the misery of millions in the rural areas and the responsibility of the Government and the well-to-do, educated urban dwellers for it that he made a passionate and unsparing indictment of their indifference and insensitivity.

'Little do down dwellers know how semi-starved masses of India are slowly sinking to lifelessness. Little do they know that their miserable comfort represents the brokerage they get for the work they do for the foreign exploiters, that the profit and the brokerage are sucked from the masses. No sophistry, on jugglery in figures can explain away the evidence that the skeletons in many villages present to the naked eye. I have no doubt whatsoever that both England and the town dwellers of India will have to answer, if there is a God above, for this crime against humanity which is perhaps unequalled in history.'

So Gandhi's concept of social reconstruction is seen to be something more comprehensive than the terms is usually taken to mean. It includes people's economic betterment, the reorganization of the educational system, the repatterning of social institutions on the basis of right moral relationships—all devoted to the *total* Improvement of the human lot which is still so miserable for the majority of mankind that it reflects little credit on man, inspite all the progress that he has made in many directions.

3

Gandhi's Concept of Culture

A superficial study of Gandhiji's concept of culture has misled many persons (including myself at one stage years ago) to the conclusion that he had a rather limited and narrow view of culture. While I have no wish to endorse in detail his interpretation of culture in all its nuances, I would venture to suggest that this opinion does him less than justice. The critics have not assimilated the inwardness of his thoughts and have failed to interpret rightly some of the basic criticisms which he made of modern western culture. It was argued that, since he had rejected many features of what was considered to be modern culture as developed in Europe and America and had endeavoured to go back to the simpler ways of living as practised in the past, he was a reactionary in cultural matters. Perhaps it would be worth while to quote some of his well-known views which support my contention. As you enter the Broadcasting House, you see a part of the following attractive quotation from Gandhi inscribed in the foyer opposite—oft-quoted, but still fresh and worthy of repetition:

> 'I do not want my house to be walled in on all sides and my windows to be stuffed. I want the cultures of all lands to be blown about my house as freely as possible. But I refuse to be blown off my feet by any. I would have our young men and women, with literary taste, to learn as much of English or other world languages as they like

> and then expect them to give the benefit of their learning to India and the world. But I would not have a single Indian to forget, neglect, or be ashamed of his mother tongue, or to feel that he or she cannot think or express the best thoughts in his or her own vernaculars. Mine is not the religion of the prison house.'

This is certainly not an exclusivist's conception of culture it does not in any way bar out that cultural traffic, that process of assimilation which has always been characteristic of Indian culture and a source of vitality to it. He is, however, anxious to ensure that this does not result in the sacrifice of the true values of our culture, that we do not become rootless in the process, developing a kind of mestizzo civilization. He made it quite clear that we should refrain from aping indiscriminately western ways of dress, speech, food and social behaviour or look upon our way of life as inferior or uncivilized because it was our own! He was all for borrowing from other cultures, provided it was done with good sense and proper selection. 'There is nothing to prevent me from profiting from a light that may come from the West. But I must take care that I am not overpowered by the glamour of the West. I must not mistake the glamour for the true light.' He had seen how, in the early stages of our confrontation with Western culture, as it came to us through the British, many of us had come to believe, like Lord Macaulay, that there was little of value in Indian languages, thoughts and culture. Gandhi tried, like some of his other contemporaries to restore our national self-respect and helped us to realise that in the process of cultural exchange we should not only take from but also give to, the West and other parts of the world. The attitude of mendicancy, the out-stretched hand is not worthy of any people with a great past, which also aspires to build a great future. 'My work will be finished if I succeed in carrying conviction to the human race that every man and woman, however, week in body, is the guardian of his or her self-respect and liberty.'

He realised quite clearly that, in this age of fast changes and quick means of communication, India was busy with evolving a culture which should be worthy of her and able to meet the new challenges of the world. It was her business to build a harmonious pattern in which healthy elements from other cultures could be wisely incorporated, provided they did not clash basically with her own healthy values and ideals. Referring to the Gujarat Vidyapeeth which owed its original inspiration to him, he elucidated this point further: 'The Vidyapeeth does not need to feed on or to repeat the ancient culture. Rather, it hopes to build a new culture based on the tradition of the past and enriched by the experience of latter times. It stands for the synthesis of the different cultures that have come to stay in India, that have influenced Indian life and that, in their turn, have themselves been influenced by the spirit of the soil'. It is not with reference the Vidyapeeth alone that he expressed this idea; he wanted it to become the inspiration of all our educational and cultural endeavour.

'The Indian culture of our time is in the making. Many of us are striving to produce a blend of all the cultures which seem today to be in clash with one another. No culture can live if it attempts to be exclusive. There is no such thing as pure Aryan culture in existence in India. What interests me is the fact that my remote ancestors blended with one another with the utmost freedom and, we of the present generation, are a result of that blend'. And then the teacher with the prophetic vision warned: 'Whether we are doing any good to the country of our birth and the tiny globe which sustains us or whether we are a burden, the future alone would show.'

It is, therefore, wrong and unfair, I submit, to accuse Gandhiji of holding a static concept of culture, which claims to have discovered and realised all that was good and noble 300 or 3000 years ago, and to which time could usefully add nothing.

While he was quite opposed to the idea of our becoming exclusivists or erecting barriers, he realised that an appreciation of other cultures can fitly follow, never precede an appreciation of our own. We must, therefore, first find our roots, discover the basic moorings of our own culture, analyse its strengths and weaknesses dispassionately and then graft on to it healthy cuttings of other cultures of the world. This attempt to understand weaknesses is important, because it is an essential condition of cultural health and growth. Those who accept every thing from the past uncritically and think that age by itself confers sanctity on an individual or institution or culture, do them great damage. Equally important is the condition of grafting only healthy cuttings of other cultures, not anything that happens to be merely eye catching or glamorous. Gandhiji accepted both these principles unreservedly: 'I do not subscribe to the view that everything is good because it is ancient. I do not believe either that anything is good because it is Indian.... I never hesitate to demolish all that is evil or immoral, no matter how ancient it may be. But.... it hurts me to think that people, in their rush for everything modern, despise all their ancient traditions and ignore them in their lives.'

One of his important criteria for judging the worth of a culture is its ability to achieve unity in diversity. A cultured man does not quarrel or fight in order to steamroll God given variety into some kind of rigidity, as many persons in history have tried to do— the big and the small dictators—but tries to look for the unity which underlies the diversity. He linked man's outer freedom with his inner freedom—the one attained by political means and often by the use of force, the other which is a result of an individual's spiritual growth and helps liberate his heart and mind. The outward freedom that we attain, he explained, can only be in direct proportion to the inner freedom to which we may have grown at a given moment. If this inner freedom is lacking or weak, political freedom may lose all its significance; for it is impossible to force freedom on any individual or organization, at least on an enduring basis.

Gandhiji sincerely believed that work and culture were intimately and inextricably related. He utterly rejected the centuries old tradition that anything connected with manual work was degrading and unworthy of a cultured man. He declared categorically: 'I pride myself on calling myself a scavenger, a weaver, a spinner farmer and do not feel ashamed that some of the things I know but indifferently. It is a pleasure for me to identify myself with the labouring classes, because without labour we can do nothing.'

His devotion to work, to action, went deep into his nature and stemmed from the depths of his moral consciousness. He accepted unreservedly Carlyle's high definition of work: 'All true work is blessed. He who has this blessedness let him ask for no other.' He put the same idea in these words.

> 'Throughout 35 years of unbroken experience of public service in several parts of the world, I have nor yet understood that there is anything like spiritual or moral value apart from work and action.'

His hole theory of basic education was derived from this belief in the value of work. He was not prepared to concede that culture only came from books. Like Carlyle, Tolstoy, Dewey, Kershensteiner and Tagore, he was convinced that, when children and adults work with their hands at productive labour and make socially useful things, knowledge, becomes highly motivated, is joyously acquired and is better assimilated and retained. It becomes a part of the worker's personality. He did not say, as many other professional educationists were saying: Let us have academic work plus manual work in schools. He stipulated that children should learn through doing, through undertaking socially purposeful activities and be encouraged to ask questions so that they may understand what he called 'the why and wherefore of things. He would have been delighted at Kershensteiner's sentence: 'The education of the worker is the door to the education of the man'. He did not, however, borrow his insight from the writings of great educationists of the world. It was derived directly from his contact with the people, from seeing the way they actually acquired the knowledge which they found most useful in life, and from their spontaneous reaction to their participation in practical activities. When, with his usual shock tactics, he put it to the Educational Conference at Wardha in 1937 that all knowledge presented to the children must come through practical work, many traditional routine bound educationists were skeptical, if not scandalised and argued that such a system would never produce a Tagore or a Raman, or a Ray when, incidentally, Tagore's own famous educational experiment at Bolpur had anticipated some of Gandhi's basic ideas.

One great advantage of his advocacy of work as the medium of education was that some educational views which had been considered quite unacceptable, acquired a certain measure of respectability. Many persons, however, accepted, or pretended to, accept them not because they quite understood or believed in them but because they came from the 'master' a compliment which he hardly relished. Handwork came into its own at least in theory and, to some extent in practice and long established traditions, which had acquired a powerful stranglehold on teachers as well as educational institutions, relaxed to some extent, the rigidity of their grip.

He envisaged education as 'the spearhead' of a silent 'social revolution' which might bring the urban and rural population nearer, break down the barriers between the classes and masses, provide a realistic education for both and thus lay the foundation for the just social order in which there is no unnatural division between the 'haves' and 'have nots'. All this has, of course, not been actually achieved but we have made some headway in this direction. As a result of the total Gandhian impact on the situation, the conflict of interests and objectives between the two classes has tended to diminish, to some extent and there are some true Gandhian workers who continue to work, often in obscurity, for the welfare of the under privileged groups.

To understand his concept of culture, we have also to take into consideration, even though briefly, his concept of proper economic life. For to him culture was not just a dalliance with music, arts and literature but part of the web and woof of everyday life. And it is only in this context that we can consider the true meaning of his criticism of the West. In this criticism, he went much further than any of his great contemporaries. He was not just dissatisfied with the lines along which Western civilization—and, following it, some civilizations in the East—had been developing during the last hundred years or more. He questioned frankly and courageously its very basis and *welt-anschauung*. He pleaded for the simple life not merely because he preferred it to the luxury and the quest for goods which were built into it, but also because he believed them to be basically antithetical to the life of the spirit. He saw the dangers of the road which civilization had chosen and warned his country men and women as well as the rest of the world against them. He agreed with Tagore that what he called the 'Thing' stifles the spirit. He advised that, so far as humanly possible, we should restrict our needs and not make use of machines merely for the multiplication of goods, many of them not of basic value to life. Particularly those who happen to possess the resources to satisfy all their wants, primary or secondary, foolish or reasonable because they are the people who set the pace for others. He believed that an uncontrolled competitive economy, based on the profit motive and by the use of unscrupulous advertisements to whet even unfelt appetites, were equally bad for the East and the West. And he was concerned about both, because in the field of social service, he made no distinctions between the foreign and the indigenous. He did not live to see the rise of the strong protest movements of the students in the West and in the East, challenging some of the basic postulates on which modern Western civilization has been built. But they do show that there was truth in his apprehension that deadly dangers lurked below its glittering facade. Dangers that have since appeared in much more violent forms than the comparatively harmless activities of the hippies, the beatles and their tribe.

His emphatic criticism of some aspects of Western culture raises several important and controversial questions. Has the advance of science and technology affected the advance of man towards humanism adversely? Is modernisation, as it has developed in the West consistent, or can it be harmonized, with the movement for the qualitative enrichment of human life? Must the acceptance of such modernisation lead inevitably to the evils associated with the normal course of industrialisation, with capitalism or totalitarianism in their various forms? Some persons have bluntly put the question. Can Gandhism set back the hands of the clock of time and revert to the simplicity of a bygone age? These are, as I said, controversial questions to which I cannot presume to give a categorical reply. But, even when we differ, we should try to understand the context and the frame-work of Gandhiji's objections. He has e.g. deprecated the use of machinery, particularly labour saving machinery, not as a matter of principle but in the special conditions in which we are living today. In a country with a population of over 500 millions, of which many millions are unemployed or under-employed and partially starving, the use of such machinery can certainly help the capitalists and industrialists to become richer, but it cannot meet directly and indirectly the immediate everyday needs of the poorer classes. He clarified the *raison d' etre* of his objection in these words:

> 'What I object to is the craze for machinery, not machinery as such. The craze is for what they call labour saving machinery. Men go on saving labour till thousands are without work, to be thrown on the open streets to die of starvation. I want to save time and labour, not for a fraction of mankind, but for all; I want the concentration of wealth, not in the hands of a few but in the hands of all. Today, machinery merely helps a few to ride on the back of millions. The impetus behind it is not the philanthropy to save labour but greed. It is against this constitution of things that I am fighting with all my might.... I would

favour the use of the most elaborate machinery if thereby India's pauperism and resulting idleness (could) be avoided.... Industrialization on a mass scale will necessarily lead to passive or active exploitation of the villagers, as the problems of competition and marketing come in. Therefore, we have to concentrate on the village being self-contained, manufacturing mainly for use. Provided this character of the village industry is maintained, there would be no objection to villagers using even the modern machines and tools that they can make and afford to use. Only, they should not be used as a means of the exploitation of others.

I have no doubt that, in this statement, expert economists can find some issues to join with Gandhiji. But while its economics, so to speak, may be arguable, its ethics is not. For him, ethics was always more important than economics, which was to be used as a means for the eventual attainment of ethical ends. He would have said: Go ahead and work out any reasonable economic system, provided it furthers the ends which I have outlined. We cannot justify an economic system, however efficient it may be technically, if it does not take into account the principles of justice and equity and does not guarantee a modicum of the good life for the masses.

This is not, however, the only gravamen of his charge against modern civilization. He also objected to its definition, explicit or implied, of what culture means. In his opinion, the unceasing multiplication of goods, their demand whetted by powerful mass-media of propaganda, is no proof of culture and no way to ensure happiness. Not only does it obscure the joys of the simple life, everyone trying desperately to rival, if not outdo, his neighbours in luxury but is also the harbinger of the serious rivalry, the cut throat competition, the accentuation of the differences between the rich and the poor which characterise modern society. 'How heavy' Gandhiji exclaimed, 'is the toll of sins and wrongs that wealth, power and prestige extract from man.' In his criticism of this cult of socially unjustified, profit motivated over production, Gandhiji is on much surer grounds. Many of the great thinkers of the West, products of this very civilization are beginning to ask themselves seriously whether their life is based on sound and sensible foundations, whether the loss of its basic simplicities and its contact with productive and socially worth-while activities and their substitution by a mad rush for speed and the crazy pursuit of wealth, really make sense? This crazy pursuit which, after a certain point, does not even mean the possession of more goods or houses or motor cars or other tangible physical and cultural amenities, but is an abstract will-o'-wisp behind which the great tycoons and entrepreneurs run like mad; not knowing whether the loss of peace and quiet and relaxed leisure and the capacity to enjoy the fruits of man's cultural effort through the ages, has been a really worthwhile return for what they have gained. This has been the philosophy of life traditionally preached and favoured in the East by many of its prophets, saints and seers. It is true that it has sometimes been preached with such exaggerated emphasis as to suggest a renunciation of the worldly life and its challenging problems and a preference for the life of the recluse. We may well find the exaggeration objectionable, but the basic truth of this view cannot be denied. Should not man try to find some point of stillness even in the heart of a storm, some area of peace even at the centre of a glowing flame?

And Gandhi's contention was that peace could only be found and life acquire meaning through service to our fellow men. In comparison with it nothing else mattered. He would neither allow 'physical voluptuousness' that is a passion for the possession of material things nor even 'intellectual voluptuousness' to come in its way. Many persons of intellectual eminence would demur so far as the latter is concerned but he wanted to make it clear that if the persuit even of high academic values lured a person away from the ideal of service, it was to be resisted. According to him, 'The satisfaction of one's physical needs, even intellectual needs of one's narrow self, must meet at a point a dead stop, before it degenerates into physical and intellectual voluptuousness.'

This is not a view of life unique to Gandhiji. There have been other great men and women in history who gave up or modified their careers in the fields of academic or cultural excellence in order to take up careers of social service. Amongst his eminent contemporaries Schweitzer is one outstanding example of a person who chose to exile himself to the wilds of Africa to bring medical help to its primitive people forsaken by civilization, rather than seek world renown, which would have been his for the asking, as a doctor or a musician.

Another apt example is that of Bertrand Russell who did not, indeed, give up his great career of academic eminence but who rated just as highly a deep compassion for the human race. In the foreword to the first volume of his autobiography, he has said with simple eloquence: 'Three passions, simple but overwhelmingly strong have governed my life: the longing for love, the search for knowledge, and unbearable pity for the suffering of mankind....I have sought knowledge. I have wished to understand the hearts of men. I have wished to know why the sun shines.... Love and knowledge, so far as it was possible, led upward towards the heavens. But always pity brought me back to earth. Echoes of cries of pain reverberate in my heart. Children in famine, victims tortured by oppressors, helpless old people, a hated burden to their sons and the whole world of loneliness, poverty and pain make a mockery of what human life should be'. Gandhiji was made of the same noble-stuff and he suffered with all the sufferers of the world.

The protest against the materialization of modern culture its growing artificiality, its exaggerated attachment to wealth and power, its piteous swing between hard work for petty objectives and escapism, its desire to dominate, its open worship of force and recourse to violence to solve not only political differences between nations but also differences between individual and groups—this protest can now be seen not only amongst the intellectuals but also, at the other end, amongst the beetles, the hippies, the flower children and other members of their tribe. One does not, by any means, agree with many of the forms in which their protest manifests itself or with the many dubious ways of escape that they seek, out of contemporary society. But one must recognise that there is a very acute sense of discontent amongst them against many of the characteristics and limitations of this highly sophisticated civilization. Gandhiji intuitively perceived of the weaknesses from which it suffered and with magnificent courage raised his powerful voice of protest against them.

'I want to declare to the world that whatever may be said to the contrary and, although I might have forfeited the regard and even the trust of many friends in the West... but even for their friendship or their love, I must not suppress that voice within, call it conscience, call it the prompting of my inner basic nature. There is something within me, impelling me to cry out my agony. You have to stand against the whole world, although you may have to stand alone. You may have to stare the world in the face, although the world may look at you with bloodshot eyes. Do not fear Khwaja Ghulamus Saiyyadain, who was born in 1904 in Panipat, Haryana, belonged to the family of Maulana Ataf Husain Hali, one of the main architects of the Muslim renaissance in the nineteenth century and a close associate of Mirza Ghalib and Sir Syed Ahmad Khan. Although Ghulamus Saiyyadain was still a child when Hali, his paternal grandfather passed away, it seems that even at this tender age he was able to unconsciously absorb much of the illuminations of the Islamic sensibility that represent the most powerful and beauteous aspects of the modern Muslim intellectual and literary tradition. Having received such a mental and attitudinal training, Ghulamus Saiyyadain was admitted in 1919 to M.A.O. College which soon became the Aligarh Muslim University, to do his graduation. At A.M.U., under the shadow of the legacy of the great intellectual giant, Sir Syed Ahmad Khan, he was introduced to an altogether different climate of ideas where the course of his mental training took a new turn. By now, he had already started spreading his wings and excelling himself in both speech and writing. His natural gifts of sharp intellect and ready wit weaved such a web of magic that both the teachers and students could not resist. Having done his graduation with flying colours, Saiyyadain found an opportunity to go to the University of Leeds, U.K. for higher studies in Education. He returned to the A.M.U. in 1925 to hold the post of Reader at the Teacher Training College. It was his initiation into a life of and in education. What started as a teaching assignment soon grew into a passion that thoroughly consumed him and became a mark of his achievement and identity. His total dedication and commitment to the cause of education and teaching resulted in his elevation to the post of the Principal, Teacher Training College, A.M.U., in 1930 when he was just 26. But even before this rise in status, he had already attracted attention of the prominent educationists in the country with his educational expertise being increasingly recognized. His reputation as an educationist was further strengthened when he was appointed to the committee on National Education, set up under the chairmanship of Dr. Zakir Husain, under the inspiration and guidance of Mahatma Gandhi. As a member of the Committee Saivyadain made remarkable contributions to the finalization of the Wardha Scheme of Basic Education. It was the highest point of his educational accomplishments and from then on his life was solely devoted to the promotion of educational theory and practice in India and abroad. During the period, he served as head of educational administration and advisor in various Indian states. He retired from active service as Secretary, Ministry of Education, Government of India. Even after his superannuation, he was not spared and made to be associated with the educational planning and other activities in India and abroad. He was also regularly invited for lectures as visiting professor at various universities the world over.

Dr. Zakir Husain was second only to Maulana Hali in influencing and shaping Saiyyadain's thought and action. He had himself admitted time and again how much he owed to

Dr. Zakir Husain for his development as an educationist and a civilizational activist. He came into contact with Dr. Zakir Husain during the preparation of the Wardha Scheme and gradually their relationship grew into a strong bond of friendship where Zakir Sahib was like an undeclared teacher. This camaraderie was not only between two individuals but also a source of inspiration for many activities initiated for the promotion of education and moral values. Dr. Syed Abid Husain once wrote about this togetherness in these words:

> From here onwards a relationship between Zakir Sahib and Saiyyadain Sahib started taking shape to reinvigorate with thought and action the educational life of new India. The educational views of these two thinkers are yet to be studied and evaluated the way they deserve. When our educationists will concentrate on their views, it will usher a new era of educational thought where Zakir Sahib will have the place of the 'Father of Education' Socrates and Saiyyadain Sahib that of the 'First Teacher' Plato.
>
> (Editorial *Islam Aur Asr-e-Jadeed*, January 1972)

Saiyyadain Sahib had a very broad, all-inclusive and holistic view of education which encompassed all aspects of life of both the individual and the society as a whole. Education for him was not merely a vehicle for acquiring knowledge or information that provides means of livelihood but a means of shaping an enlightened human consciousness and complete personality which has a sense lofty human values flowing like blood in its veins. He says:

> As we carry on our teaching assignments from day to day, teaching lessons, correcting exercises, supervising projects and experimental work, organizing games and social activities, we should be constantly asking ourselves many basic questions and taking the risk of giving honest replies: 'Are we quickening our students' minds? Are we developing their critical capacities which will turn mercilessly upon themselves but sympathetically on others? Are we enlarging

their sympathies and deepening their human understanding so that they will not think and feel and act in their narrow and dark grooves of class and creed and caste loyalties but in the daylight of national and human interests? Are we teaching them to be honest and courageous and free in their everyday dealings or implanting unlovely complexes for which they will have to suffer and pay in the long run? Can they distinguish between the beautiful and the ugly or does their education leave them aesthically blind? Have they cultivated the humble decencies of civic life which makes for harmony and cleanliness and pleasant social relations or do they continue to act in uncouth and boorish ways when they are given their head'? I dare say that these things are easy to achieve but I am firmly convinced that they are the only things really worth striving for. They alone provide the touchstone on which you can test the genuineness of the coin that you are passing on to them.

(Jha Memorial Lecture)

Mahatma Gandhi's life and views had very thoroughly impacted Saiyyadain Sahib's heart and mind. To him, Gandhiji was an epitome of the greatness of being human and civilized in the face of the forces of barbarism and violence unleashed during the twentieth century. He considered Gandhiji a one-man army of human values armed with spiritual awakening and non-violence combating the mighty forces of dehumanization. What impressed Saiyyadain Sahib the most was Gandhiji's holistic vision of life and his insistence on synthesizing the material and spiritual aspects of the human existence. Saiyyadain Sahib's educational views can be said to be an effort to translate into practice many of Gandhiji's views on education, although they were undoubtedly very firmly rooted in his own creative genius.

Saiyyadain was a firm believer in Islam and was a practicing Muslim but his vision of Islam transcended the narrow interpretations and practices that have been foisted on this great religion during the course of history. To him, Islam represented a tremendous human and civilizing force that had played a great emancipatory role during the medieval age in freeing human beings from the bondages of fanaticism, bigotry and religious exclusivism. Saiyyadain Sahib viewed Islam as a unifying universalist faith that through its insistence on the oneness of God calls for the essential oneness and togetherness of mankind. Large-hearted tolerance and peaceful co-existence were the two cardinal principles that Saiyyadain Sahib viewed as the fundamental building blocks Islam provided for raising a truly peaceful and pluralist social environment where all human beings of all creeds, colours, languages and races can live together without any friction and contributing to each other's growth as human beings.

This special issue of the *Islam and the Modern Age* which carries some important and relevant articles by Khwaja Ghulamus Saiyyadain is our humble homage to him as a great man and scholar who had made enlightening intellectual contributions to this journal.... testify to that for which you have lived and for which you may have to die.'

He was not only aware of the increasing dangers of violence in international life but also realised that violence and exploitation were permeating many aspects of national life. Supposing by some miracle war was abolished and peace established on a stable basis, it would not be enough. It will be but the starting point and the goal of a full and happy life will still be very far away. Gandhi underlined the true nature of the contemporary human situation and showed that even pacifism was not enough.

'A pacifism, which can see the cruelties only of occasional military warfare and is blind to the continuous cruelties of our social system, is worthless. Unless our pacifism finds expression in the broad human movement which is seeking not merely the end of war but our equally violent civilization as a whole, it will be of little account in the onward march of mankind. The spirit of life will sweep on, quite uninfluenced by it.'

Culture, as he envisaged it, included many qualities which had their origin in social sensitivity, the desire to share with one's fellow men the good things of life which one is privileged to enjoy. 'I hate privilege and monopoly. Whatever cannot be shared by the masses is taboo to me.' But he went further than most other contemporaries when he saw that there were many things—even essential things—which the masses could not possibly have. He simply gave them up and thus became as we have seen, Churchill's pet aversion, the naked fakir. Love and compassion were not only the most important ingredients in his culture but, in a sense, the whole of it. Love and compassion which knew no racial, religious, caste or geographical boundaries and made his heart as wide as the ocean.

'Having flung aside the sword, there is nothing except the cup of love that I can offer to those who oppose me. It is by offering that cup that I expect to draw them close to me. I cannot think of permanent enmity between man and man and, believing as I do in the theory of rebirth, I live in the hope that, if not in this birth, then in some other birth, I shall be able to hug all humanity in friendly embrace.'

In his preface to *All Men Are Brothers*, Dr. Radhakrishnan had written: 'All men are brothers and no human being should be a stranger to another. The welfare of all, Sarvodaya, should be our aim. God is the common bond which unites all human beings'. (And then with his great gift for the striking phrase, he added.) 'To break this bond even with our greatest enemy is to tear God himself to pieces. There is humanity even in the most wicked.'

Gandhi passionately hated all violence and war because it brutalizes men, even of gentle character, and often, when they emerge from it, they become incapable of leading a decent, civil life. Individual life ceases to have much value for them, for they have seen it destroyed and participated in its mass destruction over and over again. What has recently happened in Vietnam is a most horrible example of this curse and yet, I ask myself on behalf of Gandhiji whether we have any right to feel superior to the Americans on this account. There has been in the American press and public a great upsurge of revulsion and indignation at the atrocities committed by some members of their fighting forces on the civilian population and they are at present on trial not only in the courts but also in the Press. What some of our countrymen did in Ahmedabad, for instance, recently where there was no war and the people concerned were all fellow citizens was in no way less reprehensible. I have not, however, seen a similarly strong public reaction against it, nor have our mass media tried forcefully to awaken the public conscience to this enormity. How shall we answer Gandhi for what has been done and, what is far more important, God and our own conscience? Gandhi saw such things with his physical eyes and the eyes of imagination. But the wonder is he never lost faith in humanity and always cherished the hope of redeeming the most hardened sinner through his magic app-roach of love. This was an essential part of his deeply humane culture. He believed in the policy of trusting his fellow-men, preferring it to the policy of distrust and suspicion. There were risks in both, but he cheerfully preferred the risks of trust. 'One will lose nothing by believing. Disbelief is a treacherous mate. Let him beware. For my part, I am unrepentant. I have trusted all my life with my eyes open'. Thus spoke Gandhi's faith at a time when the whole of India and Pakistan was in flames in which most people's faith and decency had been burnt to ashes.

He knew that man was inventing incredibly powerful engines of destruction and death—man who was supposed to be not only the master of creation but made in the image of God. Did this shake his faith in non-violence? No, it strengthened it further. 'Unless the world adopts non-violence, it will spell certain suicide for mankind.... The moral to be legitimately drawn from the supreme tragedy of the atom bomb is that it will not be destroyed by counter-bombs, even as violence cannot be by counter-violence. Hatred can be overcome only by love. Counter-hatred only increases the surface, as well as the depth of hatred.' He elucidated this position further because it was cardinal point in his philosophy of life.

'There have been cataclysmic changes in the world. Do I adhere to my faith in truth and non-violence? Has not the atom bomb exploded that faith? Not only has it not done so, but it has clearly demonstrated to me that the twins constituted the mightiest force in the world. Before them the atom bomb is of no effect. The opposing forces are wholly different in kind, the one moral and spiritual, the other physical and material. The one is infinitely superior to the other which, by its very nature, has an end. The force of the spirit is ever progressive and endless. Its full expression makes it unconquerable.... What is more, that force resides in everybody, man, woman and child, irrespective of the colour of the skin. Only, in many, it lies dormant, but is capable of being awakened by judicious training.'

Gandhi's culture drew its inspiration and uniqueness from a rare combination of firmness in faith and gentleness in speech. It enabled him to maintain cordial and pleasant relations even with his strongest opponents and enemies. He regarded ill will as beneath the dignity of man and his goodwill to all was his strongest weapon. At the height of the non-cooperation movement, he visited the textile area in England in spite of strong advice to the contrary. In fact, many of his friends regarded it as almost an act of lunacy. But he was anxious to open his heart to the workers, for there was nothing in it to hide, no ill will, no spite, no anger, nothing but love and good-will. His initially hostile audience consisted of people who believed that he was taking away bread from them and their families. The newspapers had played up his opposition to the British and they were, understandably, in an unreceptive and angry mood. And yet, according to a reliable newspaper report: 'Gandhi's manner, marked by humour, trust, respect and compassion made it extremely difficult (for them) to oppose him'. A more emphatic testimony of his unruffled calm is provided by Romain Rolland in one of his letters written after Gandhi's visit to him in 1932. 'He could calmly answer for hours the heckling of a crowd, as he did at Lausanne and Geneva without a muscle of his face twitching. Seating on a table, motionless, his voice always clear and calm, he replied to his adversaries.... giving them rude truths which left them silenced and suffocated.'

There was no room in his concept of personal culture for the false politeness which eschews truth. Really, because a person has not the courage to speak it out, but outwardly because he does not want to offend his listeners. Such a man will often say different things to different men, either suppressing what is true or suggesting what is false, or both. Gandhi could neither compromise with truth, nor could he express it in an offensive manner. He points out:

> To say or write a distasteful word is surely not violent, especially when the speaker or writer believes it to be the truth. The essence of violence is that there must be a violent intention behind a thought, word or act.... False notions of propriety or fear of wounding susceptibilities often deter people from saying what they mean and ultimately lead them on the shores of hypocrisy. But, if non-violence of thought is to be evolved in individuals or societies or nations, truth has to be told, however harsh of unpopular it may appear to be for the moment.

Again, his concept of culture did not demand uncontrolled self-expression as is the modern tendency, but required insistence on self-restraint and self-control. In his own person, he struggled all his life to control lower passions like anger, pride, lust, greed, fear and obstinacy which come in the way of the effort to mould personality into a lovely and gracious pattern. In fact, he was convinced that, without freeing himself from these lower passions, man could not realize God. Even his journalism—an intoxicating profession which often gives the journalist a delusion of being omnipotent—was subject to the same rigorous restraint. 'To be true to my faith, I may not write in anger or malice. I may not write idly. I may not write merely to excite passion.... Often my vanity dictates a smart expression or my anger a harsh adjective. It is a terrible ordeal but a fine exercise to remove these weeds.' And how magnificently Gandhi succeeded in weeding his garden. We will find righteous indignation in his writings, but never anger or malice or spite.

In spite of his greatness, he had a degree of genuine humility which was truly amazing. We come across this over and over again in his speeches and writings—not put on, as an inverted form of pride or vanity. In fact, he regarded this humility, this ruthless searching of the self to discover personal weaknesses, as part of the essential mental equipment for a man of culture. 'In the majority of cases, addresses presented to me contained adjectives which I am ill able to carry. Their use can do good neither to the writers nor to me. They unnecessarily humiliate me, for I have to confess that I do not deserve them. When they are deserved, their use is superfluous. They cannot add to the strength of qualities possessed by me. They may, if I am not on my guard, easily turn my head. The good that a man does is more often than not better left than said.' He always measured himself against his high ideal of truth and non-violence. That is why he described himself as 'a poor struggling soul yearning to be wholly good, wholly truthful and wholly non-violent in thought, word and deed, but ever failing to reach the ideal which I know to be true.'

Gandhi was well aware of the fact that there was in the Indian tradition a tendency to exalt passive goodness, which consists mainly in carrying out a certain routine of activities and prescribed religious rituals, which were often taken as a substitute for the exercise of intelligence to analyse one's actions and unexamined doctrines and to understand the basic meaning of goodness. Having done so, people thought they had paid their debt to goodness and could devote themselves exclusively to the pursuit of worldly ends. Gandhi on the other hand, wanted to marry goodness with intelligence. 'Goodness must be joined with knowledge. Mere goodness is not of much use. One must retain the fine discriminating quality which goes with spiritual courage and character.' At the same time, he did not, like Plato, equate knowledge with virtue. He held that literary training by itself 'adds not an inch to one's moral health,' and character building is independent of literary training. What he wished to stress was not the accumulation of a great deal of academic knowledge—whose value, I think, he tended to underrate some what—but the exercise of intelligence in the solution of the problems of good and evil. He went further and warned against confusing spiritual knowledge with spiritual attainment, which men of religion have sometimes tended to do. 'Spirituality is not a matter of knowing scriptures and engaging in philosophical discussions. It is a matter of heart culture of unmeasurable strength. Fearlessness is the first requisite of spirituality. Cowards can never be moral.' Basically, however, Gandhi believed that, in the eyes of God, all human beings were equal and no one was superior to another as such on the basis of his race, creed, colour or sex. He would have rejected any scriptures which preached a doctrine of intrinsic superiority and inferiority amongst individuals because of their birth.

One of the keynotes in his concept of culture is silence. He could never envisage it as something loud or propagandist. I wonder whether you have noticed that most men of culture are soft spoken and loudness jars on them. In all that he wrote and spoke and did, he exercised economy which he once described as chastity in words, as essential as chastity in life. He would have regarded any exaggeration or flamboyancy in speech or action as repugnant to this principle of chastity. 'The dynamic force behind the great movement of non-violence is not vocal propaganda, but the silent propaganda carried on by the sufferings of the innocent victims of a cruel government.'

Unlike most public leaders in the world who cannot hear too much of their own voices, Gandhi recognized the value of both speech and silence. He saw the latter not as a negation of the former, but as having a positive value of its own. But even his 'silence day' was not for him a day of rest. He worked, wrote, planned and spent time in communing with himself and renewing his spiritual powers. He explained its *raison d'etre* in these simple words: 'We are frail human beings; we do not know very often what to say. If we want to listen to 'the still, small voice' that is always speaking within us, it will not be heard if we continually speak. Proneness to exaggerate to suppress or modify the truth wittingly or unwittingly is a natural weakness of men and silence is necessary to surmount it. A man of few words will rarely be thoughtless; he will weigh every word.'

I hope Gandhiji was right and I am wrong, but I have often observed that all over the world political and other leaders almost always seem to know what to say and many of them do not either have or hear any 'still, or small voice' and, even if it does sometime dare to speak, there is no audience to talk to!

Having observed this 'silence day' for a long time, it became for him both a physical and spiritual necessity. Originally, silence was practised by him to relieve the pressure of work and because it gave him time for writing. 'After however, I had practised it for sometime, I saw the spiritual value of it. It suddenly flashed across my mind that that was the time when I could best hold communion with God. And now I feel as though I was naturally built for silence.'

In the world of Gandhian thought, religion and culture were not strangers but closely related to each other. So much so that I have often asked myself whether a particular remark of his will elucidate better his view of religion or of culture. A cultured man to him was not one who strove primarily for his own artistic, literary or intellectual satisfaction, but one who was also concerned with the welfare of others and recognized the unbreakable continuity between the two objectives. That is why he described the concept of a good life, not in what may be called cultural terms but in primarily moral terms:

> Life is an aspiration. Its mission is to strive after perfection which is self-realization... One who hooks his fortunes to Ahimsa, the law of love, daily lessens the circle of destruction and to that extent, promotes life and love; he who swears

by Himsa, the law of hatred, daily widens the circle of destruction and, to that extent, promotes death and hatred.

Therefore, if anyone desired only his own or his community's welfare 'it can never be well with him.'

In his scale of values, small things were often great and what people generally regarded as great things were small. Many incidents in his life illustrate this point. It was partly a question of the criterion which he applied to human actions so that inevitably prizes, after which ordinary men and women ran breathlessly, had no significance for him. Partly, it was through the doing of many apparently little things in a disciplined manner that he trained himself and his co-workers for great deeds. This also explains his insistence on the purity of means as being an essential part of the purity of ends. If the means you adopt for the achievement of your ends, i.e., the innumerable small steps that you take towards your goal are good and inspired by good will, the end was likely to be good. There really is an intrinsic interpenetration between the two in the life of every human being.

It would be interesting to recall in this connection a public debate on the meaning of culture which took place between Tagore and Gandhi, who had great admiration for each other. In his inimitably lyrical manner, Tagore had written how man could derive great joy and satisfaction from the beauties of nature and art—the glorious dawn, the colourful dusk, the procession of seasons, the freshness of trees and flowers, and above all, the magic appeal of art and music. Gandhi joined issue with him gently, saying that this may well be true about people who were not, like the majority of Indian masses, famished and bowed down by the heavy burden of living. 'It is good enough to talk of God while we are sitting here after a nice breakfast and looking forward to a nicer luncheon, but how am I to talk of God to millions who have to go without two meals a day?' Commenting further, he pointed out with telling effect:

'True to his poetical instinct the poet lives for the morrow

> and would have us do likewise. He presents to our admiring gaze the beautiful picture of the birds early in the morning, singing hymns of praise as they soar into the sky. These birds have had their day's food and soared with rested wings, in whose veins new blood had flown during the previous night. But I have had the pain of watching birds who, for want of strength, could not be coaxed even into a flutter of their wings. The human bird under the Indian sky gets up weaker than when he pretended to retire.... It is an indescribably painful state which has got to be experienced to be realized. I have found it impossible to soothe suffering patients with a song from Kabir. The hungry millions ask for one poem invigorating food. They cannot be given it. They must earn it. And they can earn only by the sweat of their brow.'

One of the severest indictments that Gandhi ever made was against the comparatively better educated and well-to-do town-dwellers for what they had done to the millions of poor villagers, some knowingly some by just being indifferent to their lot. No orthodox communists indictment could have been stronger, though their language naturally differed:

> Little do town-dwellers know how semi-starved masses of India are slowly sinking to lifelessness. Little do they know that their miserable comfort represents the brokerage they get for the work they do for the foreign exploiters, that the profit and the brokerage are sucked from the masses. No sophistry, no jugglery in figures can explain away the evidence that the skeletons in many villages present to the naked eye. I have no doubt whatsoever that both England and the town-dwellers of India will have to answer, if there is a God above, for this crime against humanity which is perhaps unequalled in history.

As I see it, Gandhi and Tagore represent two equally precious strands in the pattern of Indian culture—each true in its place, each incomplete without the other. Tagore had a broad vision of human culture in which art, literature, creative sensitivity and thought found their due place. Gandhi recognized within reason that these things were significant. But he was so poignantly engrossed with *welt-schmerz*—the sorrows of mankind—so anxious to lighten their burden that art and culture and even the splendid labour of thought as such could take a back seat. Not that Gandhi did not perceive the value of art, but he envisaged it in his own terms and in the context of his total view of life:

> 'I love music and all the other arts but I do not attach such value to them as generally done.... When I gaze at the star-sown heaven and the infinite beauty that it affords my eyes, that means to me more than all that human art can give me.... Life is greater than all arts.... The man whose life comes nearest to perfection is the greatest artist; for what is art without the sure foundation and framework of a noble life?.... There is an art that kills and an art that gives life. True art must be evidence of happiness, contentment and purity of its authors.'

Tagore, likewise, had an appreciation of the economic values in life. He was also deeply interested in the improvement of the material condition of the poor. Side by side with Shanti Niketan, he established Shri Niketan which trained persons in productive crafts and he gave and honoured place to handwork in his general pattern of education. But there is undoubtedly some difference in their emphasis and their understanding of the place and range of cultural activities.

How far, one asks oneself, is Gandhi relevant to the present age? I realize that it is too big a question to be raised at the end of this lecture, but we cannot possibly overlook it. What does relevance mean? Does it mean a total, uncritical acceptance of all his ideas? To say so would be poor compliment to one who asked that his friends should wrestle with him if they disagreed with him. No, the question really is whether his ideas have any basic significance for the modern world or have become inapplicable and out-of-date. Some say Gandhi is dead in India. Is he? I do not seriously think so—though this depressing feeling does overcome me sometimes. Nor can I believe that the increase of violence in the world, since he passed away, is proof of his failure. Creative ideas have an explosive quality of their own and often prove to be 'time bombs'. In the national, as well as the world, context non-violence is even more desperately valid today, under the grim shadow of the atomic menace, than it was twenty or forty years ago. The 'lunatic fringe' advocates that even economically backward countries should produce their 'little' atom bombs—as a matter of prestige? That way, as Gandhi said, lies suicide. If this message of peace is irrelevant, what does relevance mean? India is going the way of industrialization and I doubt if anyone can stop it. But when most of the great thinkers, economists and philosophers in the West are becoming alive to its actual and potential dangers and warning the world against them, does Gandhi become outdated if he asks his people to walk warily into this danger zone? Must we repeat all the mistakes of our predecessors and pay frightfully heavy price for them before we learn wisdom?

What does Gandhi ask us to do to meet the challenges of the age and avoid its mortal pitfalls? Limit your wants and return to the simplicities of life as much as possible; eschew violence in all your personal, social, national and international relationships; do not ignore considerations of international morality when your national interests are involved, for they are not in conflict but essentially interrelated; build the economy of life on the basis of cooperation, not cut-throat competition. Is all this irrelevant today? He also insisted on social and racial equality, on raising the under-privileged groups whoever they might be, on readiness to negotiate with one's adversaries and never closing the door on any avenues of peace. Does all this sound too idealistic, too Utopian? Perhaps it is, but there is no way for man except to go on working for the Utopia, which may never come but can at least be brought nearer. If there were no dreamers and visionaries and pilgrims like Gandhi, labouring to the hill top of truth and justice, but only hard-headed self-seekers, mankind would never have made whatever progress it has. 'All true progress' said a French, writer, 'is a progress in charity, everything else being secondary to it.' Gandhi stands forth as a light house of charity in an age of growing fanaticism, hatred and violence. If he is outdated, I hope most of us will prefer to be outdated with him!

In the life of even ordinary men and women, there sometimes comes a moment of truth, which they must face in the spirit of truth or be content to die a spiritual death. The same thing applies to nations. If they continue to live a life of lies, deceiving themselves, deceiving their neighbours, deceiving the laws of Nature, deceiving their God, they may be able to thrive on it for a few decades or even centuries—for, one moment of God's time may equal many, many years of calendar time—but reality will catch up with them sooner or later. Such a moment of truth faces us today, individually as well as collectively, as it faces all the other nations of the world. I know many of us will not be able to face it with courage, because they are timid or shortsighted or selfish and self-centred. I cannot be sure whether Gandhi's India will do so. We can only strive and pray that it may, that a growing number of individuals may emerge to face their moments of truth with courage and pay the price for doing so. Gandhi had never to face it, that is, not a moment of truth, because ever since he attained moral consciousness and maturity, he was facing these moments all the time and rising to higher things over his transcended selves. In a sense, every moment was for him a moment of decision. But in his hard lived life he too had to take some heart-rending decisions which were of crucial importance to him and his country. When such decisions have to be taken, man must be prepared to walk alone and learn to ignore the advice of his friends and colleagues and the warnings of his adversaries, exposing himself deliberately to ridicule, scorn and danger. He has to do it because without doing so, he cannot live with himself or his conscience. Such a moment of decision is, in the words of an American writer, 'the loneliest in human life. It must be come upon in stillness and darkness and brooding thoughts and doubts, torn out of the deepest reaches of the soul.' Many of Gandhi's great decisions were taken in these lonely moments of agony, which were also for him moments of ecstasy.

I have often the feeling that the age-old language of man, which used words for the expression of ideas, thoughts and emotions, is ceasing to be current coin in the group relationships, national and missing fellow-citizens? Were the Sunnis and Shias in Lucknow. believers in the same God and the same Prophet, who behaved like beasts an did not even honour the sanctity of their own mosques, at all influenced by their religion or by Gandhi's humanism? The dangers of violence, against which he warned, are becoming increasingly real and we stand trembling on the brink of the precipice of ultimate disaster, many of us not even knowing that we do so. Fanaticism at a premium and tolerance, compassion and gentleness at a discount and sometimes even dismissed as bourgeois, reactionary an dispensable virtues.

What is true of India applies even more emphatically to some other countries. People who hold power or wish to wrest power from others are corrupted by it and are willing to use unscrupulous means to attain their not-so-noble ends. All this has been happening before our eyes. But power hungry politicians, all over the world, are to hard boiled and sophisticated to be unduly bothered by it. These are, they would say, part of the game of power politics—regrettable but what can we do? (And *sotto voce*, they might add to themselves.) If we are too blatantly anti-violence or anti-untruth or anti-injustice, we may lose our seats, our popularity, our power to sway the masses to our tune by playing on their lower passions. What, I ask you, can we expect of them? Gandhi would have weighed them all and found them utterly wanting and unworthy.

Again, historians with the long perspective, scientists intoxicated with their newly found power of incredible dimensions, philosophers who see civilized man as a creature, who has emerged finally as such, out of the primordial slime only some thousand years ago would say: 'What is this brief period but a wink of the eyelid in the eternity of time? After all, the Universe has been in existence for millions, perhaps billions, of years. We can afford to regard these few centuries as the teething period of man, from which he will emerge in due course, does not eternity lie ahead of him.'

I confess I am not comforted by this complacency. I would humbly reply: I do not have the good fortune to live in cosmic time. As a man I can, at the most, have a claim on about three score years and ten. Nor do I have cosmic patience. If humanity will be much better in five hundred or five thousand years, it does not give me much satisfaction today, I am more poignantly concerned with what happens to this generation and the next, with whether our lot and theirs is going to be actually somewhat better. I am a small man and to me a small visible improvement in the human condition—both material and ethical— here and now is more important than deferred payment at compound interest a hundred years hence. In this sense, Gandhi too was perhaps a small man, concerned with the material lot and the quality of life of small men and women—his eyes undoubtedly on the stars but his feet firmly planted on earth.

He believed it was possible to work for the betterment of man and to humanize him within a reasonable measure of time. It was possible to improve the world and make it a worthy habitation for this civilized man. Pessimists can find all the justification they need by looking at man's gory record, at what man has heartlessly made of man. Optimists with the urge to serve can, on the other hand, draw their inspiration by seeing how man has risen from the mire and achieved many noble things and how he can rise to still unimagined heights. Many great trail blazers in various periods of history have shown us the way. If such individuals, call them optimists if you like, did not exist in all ages and the worst apprehensions of the pessimists were well founded, life would truly be 'a tale told by an idiot, full of sound and fury signifying nothing.' But I know in my innermost being that it is not true. Christ spoke of 'the faith which moves mountains' not in the sense that the mountain will physically move, but that I, as an individual, when moved by faith, can succeed in displacing the mountain. Gandhi had such a faith. He moved many mountains. And he also had the gift of sharing it with others. His strength lay in the fact that he believed, with all his heart and soul, in *Satyamev Jayate* (truth will triumph), while most of us are content to use it only as a national motto and a slogan.

4

Gandhi's Concept of Religion

Religion was not a peripheral thing for Gandhi. It was at the very vital core of his being and the inspiration for all his activities in various fields of life. Many persons in public life are either ignorant or skeptical or opposed to religion; some try to keep their religious affiliation quite apart from their public image; some use it unscrupulously for exploiting the people and fanning their fanaticism for their selfish purposes. Not so Gandhi. He often expressed the view that, whatever power he possessed for working in the public or political field, was drawn from the depths of religious faith. For him politics was important—and could be important—only if it could be used as an instrument to advance values whose ultimate significance to him was religious. He said; 'I could not live for a single second without religion. Many of my friends despair of me because they say even my politics are derived from religion. And they are right. My politics and all other activities of mine are derived from my religion. I go further and say that every activity of man of religion must be derived from his religion because religion means being bound to God, that is to say God rules you every breath'. Ali, one of the great Imams and early Caliphs of Islam is reported to have remarked: 'If all the veils were lifted from my eyes, it would not add to the strength and certainty of my faith (in God)'. Gandhi said something similar: 'I am surer of His existence than of the fact that you and I are sitting in this room. Then, I can also testify that I may live without air or water but cannot live without Him. You can pluck out my eyes but that cannot kill me. But blast my belief in God and I am dead.' In the Quran, it has been said: 'Say truly, my prayer and fasting, my life and death are all for Allah, the cherisher of the worlds.' Interpreting, religion in the same comprehensive sense, Gandhi had remarked:

> I do not conceive religion as one of the many activities of mankind. The same activity may be governed either by the same spirit of religion or of irreligion. There is no such thing as leaving politics for religion. For me every, the tiniest, activity is governed by what I consider to be my religion.

One may raise at the outset the question: How does this fit into the secular ideology to which India is pledged under our Constitution and to which Gandhi was a party? To answer this question, we have to consider what Gandhi means by religion and also what exactly does secularism imply? If secularism means the banishment of religion from the mansion of human life, he would not favour it at any cost. But our secularism, as I understand it and as many others have interpreted it, really postulates that the State will play no favourites amongst the many religions practiced, that there will be all freedom of belief and worship, that the resources of the State will not be utilized for promoting any particular religion and that there will be no discrimination against any Indian citizen in the legislatures, the services and other fields of activity—on grounds of religion or race or class or sex. India has had amongst the great political leaders of the generation, that is now passing away, a number of distinguished men and women who were deeply religious and yet all of whom subscribed to this definition of secularism. I am sure many of you will recall that, when the Vishwabharati University Bill was being negotiated through the Parliament, a technical objection was raised, by the Law Department that the name of God could not be included in it, Maulana Azad had stated in his speech at the University: 'This sentence may find no place in legislation but is certainly has a place—perhaps a place of supreme importance—in the life of the University. I will declare with all the emphasis at my command that the objective, as defined by Gurudev, including the phrase left out in the Act, must remain the objective of your University and all its teachers and pupils. The truth is that in the three terms used by Gurudev, *Shantam, Shivam Advaitam* (Peace, Goodness, Non-duality) we have a conception of God which rises above all narrow limitations of race, religion or creed.'

When it is contended that religion should not intrude into politics, it is a warning against allowing rank communalism in the sense of communal fanaticism to become the bane of politics and using the cloak of religion to cover communal misdeeds. When Gandhiji, however, talks of religion, he is talking of something that is radically different. His view of religion maintained that it was a perpetual search for truth, that it was a force meant to unite people, to promote concord and discourage discord, that it was a recognition of the essential brotherhood of man and the fatherhood of God. He saw a basic unity running through the various religions viewed in their purity. He said: 'I believe in the fundamental truth of all great religions of the world. I believe they are all God given and I believe they were necessary for the people to whom they were revealed.' He put it even more pithily elsewhere: 'If a man reaches the heart of his own religion, he has reached the hearts of others too.' He did not identify and limit the search for God with 'going on pilgrimage or lighting lamps or burning incense or painting the image of the deity with red vermilion'. He could realise God only through wrestling, with and against, evil and through the service of his fellow beings. In his own words, 'I am endeavouring to see God through the service of humanity; for I know that God is neither in heaven or down below but in every one'. To him, it would appear to be an unacceptable command to 'render unto God things that are God's and to Caesar the things that are Caesar's,' for, in the deeper sense, he looked upon all things as God's. He did not visualise the Universe as divided between God and Caesar. Nor would he subscribe to the view that six days of the week should be devoted to the business of the world and the seventh to worship, as if they were two entirely different things. To him all days—and every moment of the day—belonged to God. This is, of course, more easily said than done and to cultivate this spirit of voluntary and joyous surrender to God's will—which all religions have stressed—requires a long and arduous discipline and a strength of faith which every one cannot cultivate. Towards the end of his autobiography, he makes a statement which explains his view of religion lucidly:

> 'To see a universal and all-pervading spirit of truth face to face one must be able to love the meanest of creatures as oneself. And a man who aspires after that cannot afford to keep out of any field of life. That is why my devotion to truth had drawn me into politics and I can say, without the slightest hesitation and yet in all humility, that those who say that religion has nothing to do with politics do not know what religion means.'

Mark these words: 'It is the devotion to truth' which has drawn him into politics, not the ordinary politician's love of power or wealth or authority. He would emphatically refute the claim that religion is meant only to cultivate one's soul in an ivory tower and is not involved, or interested, in the just solution of the world's many obstinate and heart-breaking problems. To him the object of both religion and politics was what Christ called 'the establishment of the kingdom of God on earth!' Speaking symbolically and with the simple eloquence of a prophet, he underlined the deepest inwardness of man's spiritual greatness in words which even the great Greek novelist, Kazantzaknis may well have envied:

'It is better to allow our hearts to speak for us than our words. God did not bear the cross only 1900 years ago, but He bears it today and He dies and is resurrected from day to day. It would be poor comfort to the world if it had to depend upon a historical God who died 2000 years ago. Do not then preach the God of history but show him as he lives today through you.'

He would not, however, agree with the Christian doctrine of redemption under which some one else could atone for man's sins by passing through the fire of suffering. His argument was that he did not seek redemption from the consequences of sin but wanted to be redeemed from sin itself. When Gandhi was assassinated, one of his well—known disciples, Miraben, was moved to remark: 'That sin is not of one man; it is the sin which floods the whole world from age to age and which nothing but the crucification of God's beloved can stem.' Beautifully put, but in the blood stained history of man, many of God's beloved have been crucified and tortured and put to the rack but it has not succeeded in stemming the orgy of blood which sits, like a curse on the human race since the days of Abel and Cain. Gandhi would have said, that, if you want to work for the salvation of mankind, you must change the nature of man and awaken his better self. So crucification could be one of the ways of shocking the conscience of mankind; it could not possibly solve the problem which is a much more time consuming and arduous business. Gandhiji's own spectacular death did have a sobering effect for the time being but alas, what has been happening since, in this allegedly non-violent country, makes one wonder sometimes whether Gandhi was a reality or a pleasant but incredible dream that we were just privileged to have!

Gandhi had a very sensitive appreciation of the intimate relationship between the spiritual and the secular; not acquired just intuitively but through his actual experience of working with people. He did not believe that 'the spiritual law works on a field of its own. On the contrary, it expresses itself only through the ordinary activities of life.' He had, therefore no desire to stock-pile virtuous deeds for the sake of winning merit in the world hereafter—a kind of insurance against the rainy day. Truth, love, nonviolence, service were only real when they were practiced in our every day life, here and now and helped to bring heaven to earth. As he put it, 'There is no such thing as the other world. All the worlds are one. There is no here and no there. All virtue ceases to have use if it serves no purposes in every walk of life.' It is interesting to note that we find the identical idea expressed in about identical terms, repeated by persons centuries apart, who had no communication with one another. In the Diwan of Shams of Tabrez, an Iranian poet, we find this couplet:

> I have put duality away; I have seen the two worlds as one;
> One I seek, one I know, one I see, one I call !

The whole of life, whether material or spiritual, national or international, was a unity, not divided into watertight compartments. If there is a spiritual law, if there is something like decency and truth, it must find expression in all activities of life. A truth, which echoes a well-known tradition of the Prophet of Islam: 'The whole of the earth is a mosque', meaning thereby that a truly religious person performs all his duties, whether related to religion or to the so-called mundane world, as if he were every moment in the presence of the Lord.

So this was not something unique or individual to Gandhi. Other great religious leaders and philosophical thinkers, too, have preached to a growingly skeptical world the inwardness of this relationship. It was unique in the sense that he actually tried to realize it in the uncongenial, contemporary world of the 20th century. In one of his 'Lectures on Islam' given in the early thirties, Iqbal, who was not only a great Urdu poet but also a perceptive student of religion, has expressed this truth in their thoughtful words: 'The ultimate reality, according to the Quran, is spiritual and its life consists in its temporal activity. The spirit finds its opportunity in the natural, the material and the secular. All that is secular is, therefore, sacred in the roots of its being. The greatest service that modern thought can render to Islam and as a matter of fact to all religions, consists in the criticism of what we call material or natural—a criticism which discloses that the merely material has no substance unless we discover it rooted in the spiritual. There is no such thing as a profane world. All this immensity of matter constitutes a scope for the self-realization of the spirit.'

The basic foundation of religion, as he interpreted it, rested on the twin pillars of truth and non-violence, their relative priority in that order. Truth and the unending discovery of Truth, is the goal. Non-violence is the means through which it can be attained. He held these dearer than anything on earth or in heaven—his friends, his relatives, his country. 'There is nothing on earth that I would not give up for the sake of my country, excepting, of course, two thing and two things only, truth and non-violence. I would not sacrifice these two for all the world. For to me, Truth is God. (In the Quran, incidentally, the word *Haq* is used both for Truth and for God). 'Search for Truth is search for God. God is because Truth is.' An intensity of faith which would put to shame Pontius Pilate who had asked sneeringly 'What is Truth?' and would not wait for a reply: 'There is no way to find Truth except the way of non-violence. I do not want to serve India at the sacrifice of Truth or God. For I know that a man who forsakes Truth can forsake his country and his nearest and dearest ones.' This is, no easy path, for it stipulates a life of great discipline and self-control. In the march towards Truth, as Gandhiji put it anger, selfishness, hatred etc. naturally give way; for otherwise Truth will be impossible to attain. 'A successful search for Truth means complete deliverance from the dual throng such as love and hate, happiness and misery'.' This does not obviously mean that normal human emotions cease to operate but they cease to matter to become man's constant preoccupation, when he is engaged in this pursuit. He refuses to let his conduct be dominated by them. Truth alone matters; all else, if one may say so, is moonshine. 'I would, rather', Gandhiji said without hesitation, 'wish that India perished than that she won freedom at the sacrifice of Truth.' How many of the world's political leaders including our own, can lay their hands on their hearts and say that they will never serve their country at the sacrifice of Truth or God? The moral law, according to him, is the eternal law of life which permeates the universe, in spite of the fact that, to the superficial view, evil seems triumphant. He believed that Truth and Goodness endure; evil and untruth are transitory, in spite of the brave showing that they make momentarily. Lest this should appear as unwarranted idealism on the part of Gandhi, let me remind you that the names which are best loved and remembered by mankind are not primarily the names of conquerors, military geniuses, exploiters, makers of money but those of saints and sages, the men and women of God, the founders of great religions and their distinguished followers, the poets, the artists, the thinkers, who were not concerned with violence or conquest but with being of service to mankind and winning victories of peace.

This moral law is essentially a beneficial, grace-giving law and is, according to him, mirrored in the fact that in the midst of death life persists, 'in the midst of untruth truth persists and in the midst of darkness light persists'. The powers of evil, in spite of their apparently overwhelming strength, are unable to repress permanently the gentle forces of truth and rise again and again out of the depths of man's being. It is man's duty and his glory, especially the religious man's, to strengthen and support this resurrection. From this stemmed his idea of importing conscience into public life. 'It has taught a few of us', he said, 'to stand up for human dignity and rights in the face of the heaviest odds'. Strength of numbers, which is the delight of the timid, is not an essential condition in this good fight. The valiant in spirit glory in fighting above in defence of truth and justice. It was of such that the poet has said:

> Chahti hai jab ishq ki san peh tigh-i-khudi
> Ek sepahi ki zarb karti hai kar-i-sepah.
>
> When the sword of individuality is sharpened on the whetstone of love,
> The stroke of a single soldier does the work of an army.

He also distinguished between two radically different forms of fighting, a distinction which would have gladdened Gandhi's heart:

> Kafir hai to talwar peh karta hai bharosa
> Momin hai to be-tegh bhi larta hai sepahi
>
> The man without faith relies on the sword,
> The man of faith fights without sword or armour.

He stressed the role of non-violence as being crucial in this crusade. In its negative and every day sense, it implies that one should never knowingly take life or cause pain or offence to any other person. In the positive and the more exacting sense, it demands a general attitude of love and forgiveness which takes strangers and even one's enemies within its purview. The real enemy, of the pilgrim of truth, is not the evil doer but the forces of evil and violence, of which they are often helpless instruments and which are deep inside all of us to a greater or lesser degree—all of us who presume to sit judgement on others. This is what gave Gandhiji his real humility. 'Whenever I see an erring man, I say to myself, I have also erred; when I see a lustful man, I say to my self, so was I once; and in this way I feel kinship with every one in the world and feel that I cannot be happy without the humblest of us being happy.' These are basic, moral truths, part of the precious heritage of mankind, which pass intuitively from person to person and from age to age without any written communication between them—only through the communication of vital spiritual experience. Did Gandhi know what a great Muslim saint had said in the 6th Century A.D. 'How can I sleep peacefully so long as I know that there is a single hungry man or woman in Medina?' Did he ever hear of the contemporary French author, novelist and playwright, Jean Anouilh, who wrote in his 'Restless Heart: 'However tight I shut my eyes, there will always be a stray dog somewhere in the world who will stop me being happy.' No, it is the lightning flash of compassion which makes the world's great men kin. 'I lay claim to nothing exclusively divine in me. I do not claim prophetship. I am but a humble seeker after truth and bent upon finding it. I count no sacrifice too great for the sake of seeing God face to face. The whole of my activity whether it may be called social, political, humanitarian or ethical, is directed towards that end. And I know that the God is found more, often in the lowliest of his creatures than in the high and mighty. I am struggling to reach the status of these. I cannot do so without their service. I am no master; I am but a struggling, erring, humble servant of India and there through of humanity.' This 'seeing of God face to face' may sound an unrealistic illusion in this age. It has, however, been the aspiration as well as the inspiration of millions of men of truth throughout the ages and the experience of some. A Latin inscription, carved into the stone work above the door of Professor Jung's Lakeside Villa in Zurich reads 'Called or uncalled, God will be present'. In an interview which he gave to a journalist, he stated: 'All that I have learned has led me step by step to the unshakable conviction of the existence of God. I only believe in what I know. And that eliminates believing. Therefore, I don't take his existence on belief. I know He exists.'

And yet Gandhi—this very humble and erring individual, as he calls himself—can say 'I may be a despicable person but when truth speaks through me I am invincible.' It is now not of himself personally that he speaks but of the irresistible power which resides in truth which speaks through him. Armed with this power, his ambition is to fight the evil within himself as well as his fellow men. He does not, unlike the misguided monopolists of religions, forget the real enemy within or vent his anger and fury against persons who have in any way transgressed from the straight and narrow path as they see it. He looks upon them with compassion. The great mystic poet of Islam, Jalaluddin Rumi, also spoke in his Masnavi of the real enemy which resides in all of us, more deadly than all the outward, visible, enemies:

> 'We have slain the outward enemy but there remains within us a worse enemy than he... this carnal, demanding self (*Nafs*) is hell and hell is a dragon, the fire of which is not diminished by oceans of water.'

Distressing Gandhiji's view of religion, Dr. Abid Husain has remarked. 'If man looks upon his enemies as victims of the forces of evil and treats them with love and compassion and fights courageously against the real internal enemies—passions, hatred, spite, rancour and tries to master them, he acquires the insight which enables him to see Truth unveiled'. This means that we cannot bring about a genuine transformation in others through force or violence or inflicting pain—as the world generally believes—but by gentleness, by persuasion, by suffering pain ourselves cheerfully and paying the price of our convictions. When this power has been generated not only individuals but even organized authority finds it irresistible, as Gandhi showed in his fight for freedom. If however, at any stage, it gets mixed up with violence, the grace disappears and the path becomes littered with blood and hatred and abiding ill will. Have we not experienced both, again and again, during the last thirty years? Was it not the Buddha who said: 'To every man is given the key of the gates of heaven; the same key opens the gates of hell...?'

In the matter of religion, I repeat, it is the gentleness of approach in dealing with both friends and strangers, with one's co-religionists and others that ultimately counts. This is a profound truth which many great religions share and which they have expressed in their own special idiom. Gandhiji translated the well known Sanskrit phrase: '*Satyam bruyat, priyam bruyat. ma bruyat satyam apriyam*' as: 'One should speak the truth in gentle language. One had better not speak if one cannot do so in a gentle way', meaning thereby that there is no truth in a man who cannot control his angry tongue or his angry temper. In other words, when truth has to be enforced under compulsion or gets sullied even with violence of expression, it ceases to be truth. This is also precisely the teaching of Islam. Not only '*La ikraha fiddin*' (there is no place whatever for compulsion in the matter of religion) but also as a basic principle of conduct:

Udu'u ila Sabil-i-rabbika bil hikmat-i-wal mauizatil hasana

'Call people to the way of the Lord with wise and gentle speech'—a positive command not only for the Prophet of Islam but also for all his followers.

I have referred to the teachings of some other religions, *en passant* because it is essential for appreciating Gandhi's refreshing outlook on religion. He had equal respect for the essential truth and goodness of all religions and neither showed nor felt any discrimination against their followers. If he had treated religion as dogma and identified it with a particular form of worship, he may have done so. But considering his basic concept of religion, it could not be otherwise. 'What was the meaning of saying', he asked, 'that the Vedas were the inspired word of God. If they were inspired, why not also the Bible and the Koran'—this when orthodox followers of many religions claimed exclusive monopoly in truth and God's grace ! In his own Ashram or wherever he attended a prayer meeting, he made it a point, as we all know, to have extracts read out from the sacred books of all major religions—Christianity,

Islam, Hinduism, Sikhism and Buddhism. When, during the fratricidal madness of the pre-partition and post-partition days, some members of the audience objected to the recitation of the Quran, he refused to have extracts read out from any of the scriptures. He stuck to this resolve till, in the face of his gentle but firm Satyagraha, every objector eventually withdrew his objection. His object was to bring home the fact that no person, who believed in any religion, could afford to be fanatical, that tolerance and respect for other faiths was essential for man's collective salvation. As a result of his careful study, he had found many things common in all great religions. He honoured them and asked others to do so, not merely because millions of our fellow human beings honoured them—which is a good enough reason—but also because they voiced truths which were part of our total precious heritage. 'Cleanse your hearts of all narrowness and make them as broad as the ocean. That is the teaching of the Quran and the Gita.'

Gandhi fervently believed that truth was revealed by God to many of his prophets and wise men over the ages and mankind will be poorer if it accepted some but rejected others. Addressing the Inter-Asian Relations Conference in 1947 on the 'Message of the East', he listed some of the great teachers of mankind, Zoraster, Buddha, Jesus, Mohammed, Rama and Krishna. An incomplete list, no doubt, but who could give an exhaustive list of all those whose hearts have been touched by God's lightning through the ages? He ended his speech at the Conference, saying: 'If you (people of Asia) want to give any message to the West, it must be the message of love and the message of truth'.

He had, therefore, no sense whatever of any necessary antagonism amongst the religions but held that people could attain goodness and salvation by following the essential and unsullied teachings of their own religions. In his famous commentary on the Quran, Maulana Azad has taken the same view of religion—as a continuously growing spiritual movement. In fact, Azad and Gandhi found great community of spirit between them in this, as in many other matters. Gandhiji said: 'I came to the conclusion long ago, after prayerful search and study and discussion with as many people as I could meet that all religions were true and also all had some error in them and, whilst I hold my own dear, I should hold others as dear as Hinduism. Our innermost prayer should be that a Hindu should be a better Hindu, a Muslim should be a better Muslim, a Christian a better Christian. I broaden my Hinduism by loving other religions as my own'. He recognises the identity of religious goal and the variety of paths to it. 'Religions are different roads converging to the same point. What does it matter that we take different roads so long we reach the same goal?' He applied the same acid test to the validity of all religions. 'That religion and that nation will be blotted out of the face of the earth which pin its faith to injustice, untruth or violence. God is light, not darkness. God is love, not hate, God is truth, not untruth.'

Religion, according to Gandhi, is not merely concerned with the cultivation of one's precious soul, unsullied by contact with the grim and painful realities of the world. A true man of religion must take his full share in fighting against persistent injustices. This is necessary not only because religion, at its best, stands for the establishment of peace, justice and brotherhood in the world but also because, according to him, one cannot know God except through grappling with untruth and injustice. 'I shall never know of God if I do not wrestle with and against evil, even at the cost of life itself. I am endeavouring to see God through service of humanity.' Now the most important form of this service is to fight against evil, the evil that denies to the greater part of the human race even the barest minimum needed for decent physical survival. And we have to go all the way in this crusade and not apply double standards between those whom we consider our own and others—in immorality these categories do not exist!

Like all men of deep religious faith, Gandhiji believed in the power of prayer which links a man to his maker and gives him both a sense of peace and power and the inspiration to seek Truth and Goodness and thus satisfies one of his basic needs which nothing else can. He has referred to it again and again in his writings:

> Prayer has saved my life. Without it I would have been a lunatic long ago. It has not been a part of my life as truth as been. It came out of sheer necessity, as I found myself in a plight where I could not possibly be happy without it. Three of the greatest teachers of the world—Buddha, Jesus and Mohammad have left an unimpeachable testimony that they found illumination through prayer and could not possibly live without it.

Iqbal has elucidated the significance of prayer in words which would have won Gandhiji's whole-hearted approval:

> As a means of spiritual illumination, it is a normal vital act by which the little island of our personality suddenly discovers its situation in the larger whole of life.

As he believed in prayer, so did he in fasting. Not, however, in the sense in which, since his death, it has become a means of coercion for attaining personal or territorial or group ends. Such use of fasting defeats its basic purpose of self-purification and shocking our fellow men's conscience about some great moral issue. He went on a fast unto death in 1932 to bring about change of heart among the caste Hindus towards the long suppressed Harijans. On the occasion of this fast, he wrote a letter to Miraben in which he said: 'I am glad you have understood the reason for the fast. There was no escape from it. It is both a privilege and duty. It comes rarely to some one in a generation or generations. In non-violence, it is the crowning act, if it is saturated with that spirit and the cause has no trace of self. I ask you, therefore, to rejoice with me that such an occasion seems to have come to me. I say 'seems' for my faith has yet to be tried. No one dare talk of his own strength in a matter of life and death.' He undertook another similar fast during the mad days of the fratricidal violence between the Hindus and Muslims at the time of partition. The issues were then even greater—will India remain a civilized country or will its people plunge headlong into violence and bestiality?

'Experience has shown me that we cannot be truthful and peaceful on some occasion and for some people only, if we are not so on all occasions. And, if we shall not be considerate towards one another, we shall not be considerate to the world outside. All the prestige acquired by the Congress will be gone if we are not scrupulously clean in our dealings within or without in every detail.' I quote this prophetic warning without comment.

Most of the beliefs that he cherished, whether we describe them as moral or religious or ethical, were not new. Some of them have been preached from the early dawn of man's moral consciousness. What distinguished him from many of his contemporaries and predecessors was that he plunged into the arena of politics with the legacy of these values and principles and tried unrepentantly to apply them, on a large scale, in this unpromising field. If it were merely a matter of making a fine, stirring address, President Nixon would easily score over him. Listen to this last beautiful paragraph of his great acceptance speech:

> 'Our destiny offers, not the cup of despair but the chalice of opportunity. So let us seize it, not in fear but in gladness—and, 'riders on the earth together' let us go forward, firm in our faith, steadfast in our purpose, cautious of dangers; but sustained by our confidence in the will of God and the promise of man.' These words do not mean the same thing when uttered by the normal run of political leaders and when tittered by Gandhi. For the others, they have served their purpose admirably when they have been spoken. For Gandhi, it is the deed not the word that is significant and a word not matched with

deeds is, to him, either hypocricy or self-deception. And he had, of course, the great advantage of having no ghost writers. So, whatever he wrote with his own hand came straight out of his heart.

He asked himself seriously: Is it possible to integrate moral values into politics, to resolve the clash between the material and the spiritual and subordinate the enormous power, that the growth of science and technology has placed in our hands, to the power of the spirit and the control of vision, without which, it has been said, the peoples perish? This question, which is at the heart of the crisis, through which the world is passing in this century, has also exercised the mind of many great contemporary thinkers in India and abroad—Tagore, Iqbal, Radhakrishnan, Nehru, Vivekananda, Aurobindo, Azad, Russell, Schweitzer, Einstein and others. They are agreed that life means more than the accumulation and enjoyment of material goods and comforts, that the view of civilization, as consisting in the multiplication and satisfaction of ever increasing human wants, is inadequate and wrong, that man does not live by bread alone, though bread is essential for the worlds hungry millions. Nehru, whom Gandhi described as his political heir, differed considerably from him in his view of religion. He was a great advocate of the study of science and the use of technology in order to fight poverty, hunger, disease and ignorance. But at the end of his Azad Memorial Lectures, after he had his say about science and technology, he wistfully and musingly raised the issue: 'I have no doubt that India will progress industrially and otherwise, that she will advance in science and technology, that our people's standards will rise, that education will spread and that health conditions will be better and that art and culture will enrich the people's lives.... But what I am concerned with is not merely our material progress but the quality and depth of our people. Gaining power through industrial processes will they lose themselves in the quest of individual wealth and soft living? That would be a tragedy, for it would be a negation of what India has stood for in the past and, I think, in the present times also, as exemplified by Gandhi. Power is necessary but wisdom is essential. It is only power with wisdom that is good.... Can we combine the progress of science and technology with this progress of the mind and the spirit also? We cannot be untrue to science because that represents the basic facts of life today. Still less can be untrue to those essential principles for which India has stood throughout the ages, Let us then pursue our path to industrial progress with all our strength and vigour and, at the same time, remember that industrial riches without toleration, compassion and wisdom, may well turn to dust and ashes. Let us also remember that "blessed are the peace-makers".'

Beautifully and movingly put. But Gandhi put the same thing in much fewer words when he said:

> If we have no love for our neighbours, no change, however revolutionary, can do us any good.

Gandhi was anxious to fight against the prevalent evils in society not merely because they were anti-social but because they were in conflict with the basic values of his religion and ethics. In this fight, he would not follow the dictates of expediency which rules the conduct of most politician, who would demur to taking radical steps to uproot resistant evils, because it might lose them votes or power or antagonize strong vested interests ! Buddha had once stated: 'All that is necessary for the triumph of evil is that good men should do nothing.' Also, 'When we do good slowly evil sweeps in with force.' Most good men in our country and in the world for that matter—prefer to stand apart from this struggle. Gandhi did not believe in tinkering with evil or doing good feebly. Patience with evil (like untouchability) is really trifling with evil and with ourselves. He would, for example, have deprecated the way in which anti-segregation laws are being applied in driblets to the school system in America. As a practical person and a shrewd politician, he must have realized that it would take long to change men's hearts and minds in a matter like untouchability. Yet, as I said a while ago, he shocked public conscience by undertaking a fast unto death on this issue; he wanted at least to ensure that, under law, the position of Harijans was made quite clear and they were liberated from the social tyranny from which they have been suffering for long centuries. Where his deep religious convictions were involved, he did not allow any extraneous considerations to determine his course of conduct—the fear of men the possibility that all his friends and colleagues may disagree with him or ridicule him. Sometimes this irritated them; it even brought him into occasional conflict, with them. But the conflict remained at a friendly level; it never became personal, for they knew that he had no axe of his own to grind. This eventually made for mutual goodwill and evoked respect on the part, not only of his friends but also of some of his strongest opponents.

He wanted something of the same spirit to permeate his colleagues. He once wrote in 'Young India': 'I believe we can all become messengers of God if we cease to fear man and seek only God' s truth'. Some of his companions did cultivate this fearlessness to a remarkable degree and, in moments of mass enthusiasm and, at crucial points in the struggle for freedom, even the ordinary men and women displayed it to a remarkable degree. However, it would be unreasonable to expect that they could do so all the time. Keen observer that he was, he also knew that this was the direction in which men and women must learn to move, if life is to become civilized and meaningful.

While exalting the role of religion, he also realized that religion had been responsible 'for some of the most terrible crimes in history', caused by fanaticism and failure to show tolerance and respect for other religions. Nothing, I submit, can be more despicable and wrong, than to fight and kill and torture other human beings because they call God by a different name or worship Him in different ways. This is even a more heinous crime than doing so for economic or political reasons. According to him, this was not really the fault of this or that religion but of what he called the 'ungovernable brute in man', who believed in the law of the survival of the physically fittest and not in the law of sacrifice. Gandhiji accepted the latter and rejected the former as the law of the jungle. Any civilization, based on such a law harbours the seeds of its destruction in its own bosom. 'It does not require much thinking', he pointed out, 'to know that, under the operation of the brute law of force, the modern world is pressed down with the weight of misery and affliction, inspite of the vast system of organized Government and mechanical contrivances to make men happy. There seems to be no relief unless we revert to the law of love. He pointed out that even in the life of the nations, the law of love and sacrifice has been occasionally operative. 'Christ died on the cross of Calvary and left Christianity a glorious heritage.... Joan of Arc was burnt as a witch to her eternal honour and to the eternal disgrace of the murderers....The Americans bled for their independence.' And many other similar examples can be given from the history of other nations and groups. He wanted the qualities of love and charity to be cultivated by peoples under all political conditions and he did claim, as far back as 1903, that 'we' as a people are devoted to the doctrine of non-resistance and of returning good for evil.... We consider it our paramount duty not to think evil of those who, we may consider, are doing unjustly by us. There is hardly any virtue in the ability to do a good turn to those who have done similarly by us. That even criminals do. But it would be some credit if a good turn could be done to our opponent.

However, I am beginning to doubt whether Gandhiji did not pay too high a compliment to us. Many things which have happened, particularly since he died, hardly seem to support this view. The trend towards senseless violence, selfishness, careerism, lack of integrity and efficiency in private and public life, scant regard for public good and public property, the growing belief that might is right and that almost anything can be gained at the point of the pistol or a mass agitation or incendiarism or coercive fasting are grave symptoms of social ill-health. It may be that lots of good things are happening in the country that can cheer one's heart. But, if that is so, most of our newspapers seem to have some allergy to them. To read the morning papers and observe what has been happening in India and the world during the last 24 hours is enough to sour the day. Gandhi clearly envisaged this gruesome possibility of increasing violence and warned us against the danger: 'If India makes violence her creed and I have survived, I would not care to live in India. She will cease to evoke any pride in me. My patriotism is subservient to my religion.' India has not made violence her creed but there are many people who have done worse; they have made it their practice. This is a state of things which should give our leaders and thinkers food for thought and induce agonized soul-searching. There may be something to be said for flinging stones at others' glass houses, but occasional self-criticism is not entirely out of order. Priestly has remarked in one of his articles in the New Statesman. 'Let us stop glaring at the outer world for a moment to consider our inner world reeking of mad vanity, greed, envy, jealousy, hate. Ah, if we could only demonstrate, stage our protest, raise up our white banners in those streets.' The 'us' in this refers to me, to you. to the various political parties as well as all the people and nations of the world. Gandhiji advised us to turn the searchlight inward and purify our hearts.

There was a time when some of us had the feeling, in the early years of Gandhi's leadership; that there was perhaps too much emphasis in his whole system of thought on non-violence, that there were occasions when in the defence of right, force had to be used. Any yet as events in India and the world have developed since, it seems to me that he was basically right and we were wrong. It is not merely a matter of objecting to the taking of life, which most religions share, but he seems to have envisaged, with clear foresight, that conditions were likely to develop which would threaten the survival of human culture and civilization and that it was necessary to forestall them. 'Brute force had been the ruling factor in the world for thousands of years and mankind has been harvesting its bitter fruit all along. There is little hope of anything good coming out of it in the future. If light can come out of darkness, then alone can love emerge from hatred.' The explosion of the atom bomb, which has changed for ever the shape of things to come in the world of man, was not for Gandhi merely a human tragedy, too deep for tears, but also a lesson written in letters of fire across the sky, telling man what were the alternatives open to him. He said: 'I did not move a muscle when I first heard that an atom bomb had wiped out Hiroshima. On the contrary, I said to myself: 'Unless now the world adopts non-violence, it will spell certain suicide for mankind.' But mankind, alas, still remains un-convinced, unrepentant and he was as critical of India in this matter as of the British, the Americans and others. At the time of the excesses committed by some of his own people as a revenge for the indignities and humiliating violence of the Rowlett Act, he wrote: 'A rapier run through my body could hardly have pained me more' and one knows that he was speaking the literal truth. Experience had convinced him, and reflection had confirmed the experience, that personal or national good could never be the outcome of untruth and violence. He did not primarily preach at other nations. He told his own people that the world was weary of hate and we could see the fatigue overcoming the western nations and making them feel that the policy of hate was really not worthwhile. 'Let it be the privilege of India to turn a new leaf and set a lesson to the world'. We did, it seems, start to set the lesson and then fearfully drew back and got caught in quick-sands.

I would like to touch briefly on Gandhiji's relationship with the Muslims, which has been a subject of some controversy in the past. Let me start by saying, on the basis of personal study, that Gandhiji had better acquaintance with Muslim religion and religious thought than he has been usually given credit for. I do not know whether it was due to his careful study of the Quran or his close association with Maulana Azad. Probably both. In several places in his writings, I have caught the echo of Islamic thought, even as there are clear echoes of Christianity. It would therefore be quite wrong to presume, as many Muslims did at one time, that he was ignorant of Islam or, in any way, against the Muslims. He had nothing but love for all mankind, irrespective of their religious labels and deep sympathy and compassion for those who suffered from any social, political or cultural deprivation, as was certainly the lot of Muslims in some parts of the country immediately after partition.

It is true that, at one time, he had made certain observations, particularly about the position of Urdu, to which the Urdu-speaking people, including the Muslims, had taken legitimate objection. He had said, for instance, that Urdu was the language of the Muslims, that it was written in the script of the Quran and that they could do what they liked with it. I am not quoting his exact words, but from memory. These statements do not happen to be correct either literally or in their implications. But there is no doubt that they were based on genuine and honest misunderstanding. He was a Gujarati, had spent many years in England and then in South Africa and did not have any clear idea of the linguistic situation in Northern India. Urdu is not the language of the Muslims but a true repository of the composite culture of India to which the Hindus, Muslims, Sikhs, Christians, Parsis have all contributed and, by birth it is as truly an Indian language as Hindi or Bengali or Gujarati or Tamil. It is not generally written in the Quranic script but, if it were, this could not by any means, be regarded as a point against it. Languages and scripts as such have no religion. Again, the promotion of this language, like other languages, is not the concern of any particular community but of the State and the people as a whole. However, the important point is that, when he became better acquainted with the facts of the situation and came into contact with the spoken language of the masses, it was he who fought valiantly for the adoption of Hindustani in both scripts as the official language and, when that effort was defeated by a narrow margin, he insisted on the inclusion of the genius and the idiom of Hindustani language as an essential element in the official language. He also learnt Urdu in jail voluntarily, which can hardly be cited as a proof of his opposition to it. It may be that there were other minor points on which there was misunderstanding between him and the majority of the Muslim community. We have also to remember that his general view of culture and his way of life was not palatable for many well-to-do and highly placed Muslim officials, or, for that matter for many Hindu or Sikh or Parsi officials. It did not also appeal to the pseudosophisticated bourgeoisie and land owning groups, who had been fed on crumbs from the tables of their British masters. Some of the finest and most outstanding leaders of the community, both secular and religious, were certainly drawn to him—Azad, Ansari, Ajmal Khan, Zakir Husain, Ali Brothers, Asif Ali, Sherwani, Husain Ahmad and others—and at one stage, he had also won over the bulk of the Muslim masses. But, gradually, as the political situation developed, most of them were weaned away from him partly through propaganda, which was no more honest than it generally is!

But his bitterest criticism has been on the score of his opposition to the partition of the country and what followed thereafter. Such critics seem to assume quite unreasonably that, while he could have criticised the Hindus if he wanted to, he should have left the Muslims quite alone, treating them as sacred territory. No one, who had any inkling of the way in which his mind worked, could ever insist that he should exercise an act of self-denial with reference to any particular community. To him, the Hindus, Muslims, Sikhs, Christians, Harijans, the British were all alike. He did not show any special consideration to the Hindus and sharply criticized them when they went wrong. Acts of murder, loot, arson and bestial cruelty were going on in India and Pakistan and he was the first to raise his voice of protest against them all and to say: 'Madness answered with madness simply deepens it; it never dispels it. Hinduism will be sorry stuff, if it has to exist on cowardly vengeance that pursues those who can offer no effective resistance.' He had also hit hard at Hindu society for having hugged untouchability to its bosom for thousands of years. 'Has not a just nemesis overtaken us for the crime of untouchability. Have we not reaped as we have sown? We have segregated the 'pariah' and we are in turn segregated in the British Colonies... untouchability poisons Hinduism, as the deadly drop of arsenic poisons milk.'

Would it be right and reasonable, I ask, to expect Gandhi to criticise the mistakes of the Hindus and to say nothing about the mistakes of Muslims of India and Pakistan? This course of action could only be adopted, either by a coward or by someone who was interested only in one community and not in the others. And Gandhi was neither. He saw it as his duty to condemn evil and violence and hate wherever he found them, whatever the religious labels under which they paraded themselves. It did not matter to him; it should not have mattered to him whether the Hindus or Muslims liked what he said. His touchstone was his own conscience, his still small voice, his deep religious urge—and not public acclaim. He was not afraid of speaking out the unpopular truth and, if he had held his tongue about the misdeeds of the Muslims, I for one would have doubted whether he was their true friend. And surely he had the right, as all of us have the right, to hold his opinion about the division of the country. To give this right to every ignorant, unlettered villager and to have a grudge against Gandhi for having exercised it, seems to me the height of unreason.

But he did much more than demonstrate his friendship by his frank criticism and by treating Hindus and Muslims alike. When the time of suffering came for the Muslims after partition,

Gandhi rose magnificently to their defence and staked his life on the issue of Muslims being able to live honourably in India. His post-prarthana speeches, which were broadcast on the AIR, will be reckoned as constituting one of the finest documents of humanism. 'I regard myself as a friend of the Muslims. They are my blood brothers. Their wrongs are my wrongs. Any evil deed done by a Muslim hurts me as much as that done by a Hindu. We may not gloat over the errors of the least of our fellows'. He wrote in the Harijan in 1946: 'We must not cease to aspire, inspite of wild talk, to befriend all Muslims and to hold them as prisoners of our love,' and a few weeks before his death, in one of the post-prarthana speeches, he reminded his predominantly Hindu audience: 'Delhi is poorer for the disappearance of the exquisite workmanship of the Muslims. It is a miserable and miserly thing for the Hindus and the Sikhs to take away from them their means of livelihood.... In this great city of ours there is room for all.... The condition of keeping me in your midst is that all the communities in India live at peace with one another, not by the force of arms but that of love than which there is no better cement to be found in the world.'

When some of the vociferous champions of the community had wended their way to Pakistan, leaving the Muslims in India to their fate, it was the humanism and sense of fairness of men like Gandhi and Nehru which came to their rescue and, at considerable risk to themselves, they laboured to quench the flames of fanaticism and hatred which excesses on both sides had nourished into an all-consuming fire. Did I say, 'at considerable risk to themselves'? No, in the case of Gandhi, it was something much more dramatic, much more poignant, much more moving than a question of risk. He welcomed the assassin's bullets on his bare chest, as a 'punishment' for showing his sympathy for the Muslims and to pay the price for his goodwill to Pakistan, although it had been created inspite of his opposition. He used his immense moral authority to have fifty-five crores of rupees paid to

Pakistan, which India owed to it. He was planning to undertake, in Pakistan, as he had done in India, a village to village peace march, which may quench the flames of communalism there; he wished that, on the gates of Pakistan, may be inscribed, with justice, (I repeat may be inscribed with justice), the verse written in the Delhi Fort: 'If there is a paradise on earth; it is this, it is this, it is this.' Does this show any feeling of ill will towards the Muslims or to Pakistan? And then this man to whom all mankind was dear, who wished well to all other peoples and countries, stood the supreme test, when it came, with courage and dignity. 'Greater love hath no man than this that he lay down his life for his friend.' This spectacular demonstration washed away all the poison that years of propaganda had generated and, at lease for once, the whole world Hindus and Muslims, India and Pakistan, East and West—stood together to honour the memory of the greatest man of religion and peace that this country had produced in many centuries. The programmes put up by the Pakistan Radio, on the occasion, were at least not inferior to those put up by the AIR. But no one, on either side of the border, capitalized imaginatively on that tragic but glorious moment. Time that creates also destroys; time that etches its message on the heart can also erase it, pushing it away into the eternity of oblivion. The moment stood stark still like a beacon of light, as if waiting for a noble response and was then plunged into the tempestuous darkness of unchaste politics, whose bitter fruit we still taste.

In 1958, the Unesco published in honour of Mahatma Gandhi a selection from his writings called 'All men are brothers', giving attractive glimpses of his life and thought. Many of you must have had an opportunity of reading it. The title provides the key to the basic core of his teaching. There was also published, some years ago, on behalf of some organization in U.S.A., a small folder entitled 'Declaration of Brothers'. I do not know its source; I do not know if Gandhiji had ever occasion to see it. If he had, I feel sure he would have welcomed and endorsed its basic philosophy unreservedly, because it sums up his own deep humanism, his compassion, his religious faith. I should like, with your permission, to read out four stanzas from it in the hope that in your hearts you will say Amen:

> We speak:
> Sons of God:
> Black and white, red, brown and yellow—men of all nations;
> The halt and the hale;
> The filled and the empty; the naked and the clothed;
> The builders of buildings, dreamers of dreams —
> Women, too, and youngsters still growing;
> All sons of God;
> All brothers in our deep currents.
>
> I said: Hold my hand; we shall walk together;
> We shall destroy fear, you and I;
> We shall fill the empty ones and ease them who suffer; we shall strengthen the feeble; the tyrant shall flinch from us; we shall impart knowledge;
> And feeding them, be fed; and healing them, be healed. So shall we profit, the one by the other;
> For we are the sons of God;
> We are brothers in the deep currents.
> Surely, where one rests, his brother may rest also;
> and where one eats, his brother may break bread;
> there shall be no discrimination between us.
> Nor will I impede your passage across my country;
> What I have is here; see it, go home and tell them;
> 'Ore in the mines, so much; and factories and farms;
> yes, and in that country such and such thoughts;'
> Send me your bales. I will buy them, and send in turn;
> we will exchange freely according to our needs.

Seek forthrightly your particular good; I will help you. The labourers shall gather together for their good, and the farmers, and those who buy; and the children shall gather in the schools; with none favoured; all for their particular good;
All brothers—our children too brothers;
For it was said, 'No man lives to himself, and no man dies to himself; but living or dying, we are the Lord's and each other's.'

Therefore we speak;
Sons of God:
Brothers in our deep currents.
We say to our leaders, Lead us in the ways of love and reconciliation, and we shall follow;
We shall toil up the steep slopes,
If need be, all our lives long, and barefoot if need be;
Till we greet the day of justice and love, the day of freedom from fearing.
'This is our pledge and our contract—
The black and the white, the red, the brown and the yellow, men of all nations—
This is our pledge to our Father.

5

Gandhi's Lovable Personality

It is particularly appropriate that, in this year of Mahatma Gandhi's Centenary, the Patel Memorial Lectures should be devoted to the study of some aspect of his life and thought. This would have gladdened the heart of Sardar Patel who worked valiantly, with him and after him in the service of the country and left the impress of his vigorous personality on many aspects, of our national life. Gandhi has made a unique impact on the mind and heart of his age, although many of the values which lie deeply cherished were—and still are—at a great discount in the world. This is a good opportunity for us to assess some of the results of this impact as objectively as possible and to examine his relevance to the modern world. There are many persons—not all, by any means, his detractors—who sincerely think that the Gandhi era is over. They recognize that he provided brilliant leadership in the fight for freedom—as well as in many other fields, where results are neither easily perceptible nor quick to mature—but, having done that, his role has been completed and many of his teachings are not really valid now either for India or the world. We would do well to recognise this new trend, particularly in the younger generation which did not have the stirring experience of actually seeing him and coming under the spell of his personality. Is this a really correct and complete assessment? I hope to examine some facets of this criticism in the course of these lectures.

While I appreciate the relevance of this theme to the occasion, I do not quite know why I have been chosen for the honour. Some of his friends and co-workers are luckily still alive, a few of them present in this hall—who had known him longer and more intimately whereas I came into contact with him mostly in the last decade of his life. They could have done fuller justice to the theme and spoken with greater authority. Also, only last December, Shri Shriman Narain, one of his close co-workers arid a careful student of his thought, had spoken on a somewhat similar theme. This, is indeed, good but you will agree that this does rather queer my pitch! However, I am grateful for this invitation because it has led me to a restudy of Gandhi's writings again and this has been an enriching spiritual experience.

During the last fifty years, so much has been spoken and written about him and he has himself written so much about his ideas, his values and the course of his spiritual growth that it is difficult to find something original to say about him. Original ways of doing so, yes; original interpretation of his ideas possibly, but originality of content, hardly, unless, of course, like Arthur Koestler, who has the dubious gift of being able to see 'darkness at noon', one set out to prove that India would have been a better and healthier country if Gandhi had not existed! However, having been offered the challenge of this responsibility and having accepted it in a moment of mental illucidity, I shall endeavour to do my best. As you know, my first lecture is entitled 'The lovable personality of Gandhi', the second 'Gandhi's concept of religion' and the third: 'Gandhi's concept of culture', I consider the last two to be particularly significant facets of this thought, both for India and the rest of the world. I have not considered it necessary to elucidate his political and economic ideas because they have already received adequate attention and their roots really lie in his religious and cultural ideas.

The best commentary on Gandhi is provided by Gandhiji himself and therefore I have preferred to rely mainly on his writings and speeches and made them the starting point oft my thinking. Particularly his deeply moving autobiography,

My Experiments with Truth which provides an authentic account of his chequered unfolding told with a courage, simplicity and frankness rare in such documents of personal history. Many years ago I had read the book and it gave me a glimpse of his mind, simple and intricate, modern and yet steeped in tradition. Some months ago, when I was in Canada, I happened to read it again and it opened new vistas which I had missed at the first reading. Perhaps this is true of all great books; they do not yield their full treasures without the labour of thought and some assimilated experience of life. In the very introduction to the book, he has set the mood needed for its understanding:

> It is not my purpose to attempt a real autobiography. I simply want to tell the story of my numerous experiments with truth and, as my life consisted of nothing but these experiments, it is true that the story will take the shape of an autobiography... I believe or, at any rate, flatter myself with the belief, that a connected account of all these experiments will not be without benefit to the reader. My experiments in the political field are now known not only in India but, to a certain extent, to the 'civilized' world. For me, they have not much value and the title of Mahatma that they have won for me has, therefore, even less. But I shall like to relate my experiments in the spiritual field which are known only to myself and from which I have derived such power as I possess for working in the political field. If the experiments are really spiritual then there can be no room for self-praise. They can only add to my humility. The more I reflect and look back on the past, the more vividly do I feel my limitation.

As I read about these experiments, their successes and failures, the groping towards and discovery of truth, and about his prolonged struggle with himself and how he forged the gem-like purity of his personality out of what seemed rather ordinary and unpromising material in the beginning, I came to see something of the epic grandeur of his development and to realize that this was no ordinary person. Here was a man who was working on himself as a jeweller works on an uncut diamond. Also, he was extraordinarily introspective and self-critical. He judged himself as ruthlessly as I was going to say as others, but I cannot do so because he judged them not ruthlessly but compassionately. So, how shall I put it? While he judged others compassionately, he judged himself as ruthlessly as if he were a criminal before the bar of his own conscience, of the still small voice which continued to whisper to him all his life, till it was strong enough to drown the cacophony of world noises.

I thought of many of his great contemporaries—Tagore, Sapru, Nehrus, Das, Azad, Ansari, Ajmal Khaṇ, Sarojini Naidu, Patel—who were, so to speak, to the manner born—scions of great families, usually with first class education and cut out for the role of leadership by their heredity, their environment and their personality. On the other hand, you look at the early or even middle age photographs of Gandhi, you see no Apollo-like beauty, no charisma, no clearly discernible signs of his destined greatness. Even in his personal appearance, you see the miracle of the spirit gradually permeating and transforming matter. The recruit in the ambulance corps of the Boer army or the barrister who started practice in South Africa might be any one. But look at some of the photographs of his later years—I am thinking of one photograph in particular, with a far away look in his eyes as if communing with God and the thoughtfulness, the composure, the compassion of Buddha in the face. What a difference!

His whole life, as he said, was thus 'a continuous experiment in the search of truth. He was always seeking, always learning, always ready to learn. As he has pointed out in his preface to *The India of My Dreams*: 'I am not at all concerned with appearing to be consistent. In my search after truth, I have discovered many new ideas and learnt many new things. Old as I am, I have no feeling that I have ceased to grow inwardly.' So, weighing every step he took, in the political as well as in other fields, in the scale of moral values, he grew not only in mind, which is not so rare, but also in the power of the spirit, working out an amazing harmony in what are usually considered discordant elements in most men's personality.

His main inspiration in life was God as he conceived Him but he realized early that, after God, the source of power and inspiration for work lay in the people, whose service was his life's highest ideal. He could not serve them fully unless he was able to identify himself with them completely, to such an extent that they could irresistibly feel one with him. He attuned himself, in his way of life, to the deprived, the exploited, the poor, the hungry, the ignorant, the *daridranarayana* who consituted the large majority in the country. He had seen that most of the national leaders, in the early decades of the century, lived a life which was as a rule, quite cut off from the life of the masses. They did not speak in their language or dress like them or live in their style and were not really concerned with their problems or their moving and miserable condition. They were more concerned with the protection of their individual and class interests. Gandhiji changed all that. A man of the people, he equated himself with the people—quitely, passionately, sincerely without the fanfare claims which the later champions of the poor and the exploited have made fashionable. He deliberately reduced his standard of living to that of the poorest and the lowliest so that they may look on him as one of themselves and may feel no hesitation in opening their hearts to him. The irrepressible and well beloved Sarojini Naidu did once say, with her waggish humour, that 'it takes a great deal to keep Bapu in poverty'. But no one can deny that he ate, dressed, travelled and lived as an ordinary poor villager would and managed to control completely the urge to seek physical comforts and carefully cultivated the capacity of non-possession. 'As days went by I saw I had to throw over-board many other things which I used to consider as mine and a time came when it was a matter of positive joy to give up these things.... Exploring the cause of that joy, I found that, if I kept anything as my own, I had to defend it against the whole world.' So acute was its sense of kinship with lowly that, speaking at a Conference of Suppressed Classes at Ahmedabad, he declared: 'If I have to be reborn, I should be born an untouchable so that I may share their sorrows and suffering and the affronts levelled at them, in order that I may endeavour to free myself and them from that miserable condition.' When he was going to attend the Round Table Conference in London, in 1931, he was asked by a Customs official at Marseilles, whether he had anything to declare he replied: 'I am a poor mendicant. My earthly possessions consist of six spinning wheels, prison dishes, a can of goat's milk, six homespun lion cloths and towels and my reputation which cannot be much.' He, of course, forbore to declare, out of modesty, that he also carried within him a dangerous heart which was open to the joys and sorrows of the world! That is why, he also remarked 'My soul refuses to be satisfied so long as it is a helpless victim of a single wrong or a single misery. But it is not possible for me, a weak, frail, miserable being to mend every wrong or to hold myself free of blame for all the wrongs I see'. Inspite of this, he set to himself the magnificently impossible task of 'wiping every tear from every eye'. In this process, he not only *gave* to them but received from them—their unbounded love, their admiration and trust, the courage to fight *for* them against all vested interests and *with* them, when necessary, for their own good and from them he drew the inspiration for all his programmes and policies.

There have been many other individuals in history who had great reserves of spiritual power, which they cultivated assiduously but, having done so, they often developed into self-centred persons, concerned with their own salvation and riot preoccupied too much with the sorrows of their fellow men. One respects them and is some times awed by them but they do not move the inner chords of our being. We have the feeling that they are not ordinary mortals like us; they do not provide the kind of example that we can well emulate. Not so Gandhiji. He was essentially a very humane person, gentle, modest, affectionate, humorous, ready to talk to every one, to listen to every one, never giving the impression that he considered you inferior and himself superior. And he enjoyed jokes against himself heartily. In fact, he had need for this sense of humour—in order to preserve his balance and sanity in his own country and the world—both of which were passing through the most traumatic and soul-shattering experiences in his life time—and still are. Once an American journalist, who was perhaps trying to score a point off him, asked somewhat cheekily 'Mr. Gandhi, do you have a sense of humour?' He looked at him quizzically for a while and replied; 'If I had no sense of humour I would have committed suicide a long time ago!' Personally, I place this sense of humour quite high in the list of human qualities; for, a person who lacks in it, is apt to become pompous, inflated, placing his image on a high pedestal, worshipping it and hoping 'that others may do the same! We have such specimens in our public life, in our services and in the money market. We will all be healthier, if we could take a leaf or two in this matter, from Gandhiji's book.'

Gandhiji's supreme quality, 'however, was his all embracing humanism which did not recognize the usual categories of the high and the low, the rich and the poor or of the religious or political labels which men and women wore, or the caste names under which they paraded themselves or suffered their 'fated' ignominy. He called himself a socialist and defined socialism as a social order in which 'the prince and the peasant, the wealthy and the poor, the employer and the employee are all on the same level. Looking at society all the world over, there is nothing but duality or plurality. Unity is conspicuous by its absence. But, in the unity of my conception, there is perfect unity in the plurality of designs. Let us ask ourselves how much we have done to identify ourselves with the masses? Have we bridged the gulf between the surging millions and us? To what extent do you share the life of the masses? I confess that with me it is still an aspiration.'

Gandhiji had no favourites—except those who strove with him in the service of truth: no favourites except those who laboured to banish injustice, exploitation and religious and racial fanaticism and fought against them under the banner of Ahimsa; no favourites except the weak, the downtrodden, the Harijans whom society had been treating as its accursed stepsons, who had neither self-respect, nor work of significance to do, nor even the basic minimum of one full meal a day. So, in a sense, the whole world was his favourite except the killers, the exploiters, the clever manipulators in different fields of life who gambled with the happiness and welfare of individuals and groups for their own petty and mean purposes. But—and this is a significant but—while they were not his favourites, he was deeply concerned about them also and anxious to redeem their souls. He sincerely believed that there was some spark of goodness, some hidden flash of the divine light in every human being, however, depraved. In his deep compassion he could see the tiny spark of divinity even in the worst criminal. And he considered it his business to awaken it at any cost. In fact, one may almost say that he regarded this class of persons also with all their special privileges of wealth and position as under-privileged—that is, spiritually under-privileged. While the others had little or no privileges, these were twice unblessed-they had many kinds of privileges but they did not use these for the good of their fellow men and women. And unshared, selfish privilege is really like an grindstone round a person's neck. They only fattened, and thus morally killed, their own egos. Selfishness clarified them. Like Daniel Webster, the fabulous American lawyer, he was prepared to wrestle for their souls with the Devil himself, and, if he could do so successfully even for one misguided soul, he would regard it as a great moral victory. This is, if I may say so, the great difference between the way of the politician and the prophet, the power drunk maniac who has the presumption to remake the world in his own image, to treat it as an instrument of his unchaste will and the patient, loving, heart-breakingly difficult way of the man of faith (the *Momin*), who knows that he is not God but only a humble instrument of His will, who can fulfil his role, only by trying to serve God's increasing purpose and not his own increasing thirst for power or wealth or worldly goods or his desire to impose some sort of uniformity on his fellow men which is so dear to the heart of the bureaucrat, the technocrat and the new God, the computer.

It seems somewhat presumptuous to intrude the first person singular in this lecture but this is the only way in which I can attempt to bring home to the younger generation and to all those who did not have the privilege of seeing him in the flesh, the extraordinary warmth and humanism of the man, which put every one at ease effortlessly. I saw him for the first time when he visited the Aligarh University in 1920 at the beginning of his non-cooperation movement and issued his famous call to the staff and students to quit all educational institutions run or sponsored by the British Government which, he said, was an anti-national and tyrannical Government based on violence and untruth. He asked them to establish 'National Institutions', independent of Government, and suggested that surplus students, for whom such institutions were not available, should do national service of various kinds. His knowledge of Hindustani was then quite meagre; he spoke haltingly, trying to find the right word and his accent seemed droll to his pseudo-sophisticated audience. He could have spoken in English over which he had much better mastery but he deliberately preferred to use the Hindustani medium because it was part of his basic programme to do so. Even then, young and immature as I was; a 1-year student, I felt that here was a man who, inspite of his broken and hesitant speech, spoke every word from the depth of his heart and meant everything that he said. You could agree with him or disagree with him but you could not doubt his sincerity. He made his speech to a somewhat indifferent audience, many of whom did not see eye to eye with him because their political and economic background and affiliations did not predispose them to accept his radically new doctrine of non-cooperation. And they were not really much to blame, because that was then the dominant mood of the country and in particular of all those who, had any vested interests in the existing Government of the country. They were not, so to speak, conditioned to respond to him affirmatively. And yet how surprised I was the next day, when the students held a follow-up meeting of their own to consider his appeal and some of the best and most sensitive students decided, against all counsels of worldly wisdom and the pressure of parents and political authorities, that they will snap their fingers in the face of the Government and throw in their lot with this 'crazy' man! He did not possess any of the superficial paraphernalia of the traditional type of leader. And yet their hearts responded to the appeal. Amongst them was a young and brilliant post-graduate student, Zakir Husain, who provided a rare quality of leadership for the dissenters. He faced his 'moment of decision' with a courage worthy of a true disciple of Gandhi, came to a fateful decision and then never looked back wistfully to what he may have missed in life. A decision which carried him ultimately, through long decades of poverty seasoned with the thrill of creative work, to the highest position in the country. This was the first time that I saw Gandhiji and heard him as one of a thousand students and the impression never faded.

For many years thereafter, I had no personal contact with him; though occasionally I heard him speak, I read about him and studied some of his writings I did, however, have a chance in the meanwhile, to meet some of his close personal friends and colleagues. I used to wonder what there was in this frail man which attracted so many of his brilliant contemporaries, each distinguished in his or her own way and all willing captives of his mysterious charm and power. Arguing with him, disagreeing with him, sometimes quarrelling with him, some of them even being irritated by his unique amalgam of religion, ethics, economics and politics, but never able to break with him, never able to walk out of the spell of his moral authority or deny his shrewd political sense, kind of a sixth sense rooted in the depths of his spiritual being. And more and more came under this spell as the years rolled on—politicians, princes, public men, business magnates, intellectuals, rich men, poor men, men who were religious, men who were anti-religious, Indians, foreigners. As a Persian poet has said:

> All the deer in the desert have flocked together with their heads on their palms.
> In the hope that per chance he may come one day to hunt

Thanks to Dr. Zakir Husain, I came into personal contact with Gandhiji in 1937. He had convened the first National Education Conference in Sevagram and placed his ideas on education before a gathering of distinguished educationists belonging to different schools of thought. These ideas had a mixed reception, as was to be expected, because he had his strong, individual point of view which did not fit into the grooves of traditional thought. Some welcomed them enthusiastically as coming from the 'Master', some opposed them strongly because they could not envisage education in his terms at all and some gave their discriminating and tempered support. It was Dr. Zakir Husain who stood out in the whole group, agreeing with Gandhiji in many of his basic ideas, joining issue with him on some points and giving the discussion a fruitful and academic, rather than a narrowly political turn. It is not my purpose to give here a history of that fateful conference but to refer in passing to some of its results. Quick to recognize merit, Gandhiji appointed a committee of educationists, with Dr. Zakir Husain as its Chairman, charged with the responsibility of translating his general ideas into educational terms. At his instance, I presume, I was appointed a member of the National Educational Committee. I was then working as Principal of the Teachers Training College at Aligarh, with a great deal of interest in and some knowledge of the activity movement in education and the ideas of educationists like Dewey, Kerschensteiner, Adolphe Furrier, Tagore and others. The membership of the Committee took me several times to Sevagram where I was able to spend days in the world of Gandhi which was, in some ways, a new world to me. There I saw how he was not merely a leader of men, but also a man of extraordinary organizing ability, who made the fullest use of every moment of his own time and every trace of ability and promise that he found in others. He responded to people's needs with a kind of sympathetic intuition and his own high ethical standards did not come in the way of understanding their weaknesses and failures. The exacting, monastic, puritanical atmosphere of his Ashram was transformed by the warmth of his personality and winsomeness of his smile, from which his missing teeth detracted nothing and the infectiousness of his artless humour which broke through formality and established the common human touch between him and his audience.

Our work as a Committee, was finished within about three months and an expenditure of a few hundred rupees, a somewhat different dimension of time and money from most other committees and commissions. During its various stages, we talked to him placed our difficulties and differences before him and he always showed in discussion the incisiveness of his mind, his vision and insight based on—first hand experience, as well as the reasonableness of his approach. Not apologetic about his opinion, but ever ready to consider other points of view. He would give his views firmly but not dogmatically and would always be amenable to reason, anxious to examine pros and cons and willing to compromise, whenever he saw justification for doing so, provided no abandonment of his basic principles was involved. In these discussions, I remember disagreeing with him sometimes, at first hesitantly and, later, as I came to know him better, more frankly. He never slighted or, in any way, snubbed, any expression of opinion—in fact he always welcomed all honest differences. He showed his human side best in dealing with small, every day problems and looking after his guests and visitors with care and affection. When I came to stay in Sevagram for the first time, he asked me: 'Are you quite comfortable?' I said 'Yes'. Having noticed some reservation in my tone, he asked smilingly: 'But you seem to hesitate in saying so. What is it?' I said, 'Yes I have one small inconvenience. I get no tea in the morning or in the afternoon.' I knew of course, that tea was not usually served in Ashram. He grimmed with a twinkle in the eye, turned to Aryanakayam and said, 'Did you hear this? From this afternoon, you will have to arrange tea for Saiyyadain'. A very small incident but it shows that he was no fanatic, he did not desire to mould every one in his image; he knew that persons have different tastes and there is no justification for imposing any one pattern on them—except, of course, on such inmates of his Ashram as voluntarily chose to tread his thorny path.

When the report of the Basic Education Committee was complete, the members went to Sevagram to present it to him formally and he said some encouraging words of appreciation to the Committee. I remarked that we had been able to do the work so quickly because of the inspiration and leadership we had received from our Chairman. He turned to me and said '*Magar, Zakir Sahib to kahatay hain ki unkay pichhay shakti apki hui*' (the power behind him is yours). I did not know anything about it and felt embarrassed and tried to parry the compliment by saying that this is just what one would expect a gracious person like him to say. But he would not give up his ground and replied: '*Zakir Sahib kabhi ghalat nahin kahtay*'. Again, a very small incident but it throws light on the greatness and gentle humanism of this man who will go out of his way to encourage even comparatively unknown younger persons and help to build up their morale. As Nehru said more than once: 'We were but small men. He picked us up, made us part of a great movement and something of its greatness pressed into us'.

He was a hard task master and would not be satisfied if any one did less than the best he was capable of. He ensured this primarily by doing more than his colleagues and by applying stricter and more unsparing standards to himself. He did so much work every day—and its range and variety were really amazing—that his colleagues would have felt instinctively ashamed of themselves if they failed to emulate his example. He 'drove' them to it but only through the pull of their conscience, their sense of duty and his own compelling, personal example. He always had a full daily time table every moment parcelled out for a particular task. He was meticulously punctual and valued time far more than most of his countrymen and women. Important Indian and foreign visitors, a whole stream of them, would come to see him everyday, mostly by appointment and during the allotted time he would give them his full attention. But as soon as the time was up, he would look at his watch, put on his irresistible toothless smile and say good humouredly: 'Now your time is up' and the most important of the V.I.P.'s would take it from him with a good grace and hasten their departure. Even on his weekly 'silence day', the only thing he did not do was to speak. How much all of us would profit if we could have one day (or even more) in the week when we would give rest to our tongue, which is so apt to run away with our judgement and discretion. Gandhiji was no rigid doctrinaire. He did not initiate a new cult or a new religion and would not call himself a Gandhian. His message of love and non-violence, he claimed, was as old as the hills and as fresh as the morning's dew. He was governed in his conduct by his deep moral convictions to which he owed unflinching loyalty. He carried on a dialogue all his life both with his friends and adversaries with good humoured patience, never losing his temper, always ready to make compromises where he felt they were called for. His opponents must have sometimes found this 'sweet reasonableness' very trying for they could not often help being disarmed by it!

We, who honour him, would do well to avoid the danger of importing literalism in interpreting his teachings—'the Master' has spoken thus; we must follow him to the letter'—forgetting that the letter often killeth; it is the spirit that keepeth alive. He would himself have advised us—did, in fact, do so—to assimilate the basic essentials of his thought and not to be concerned too much with detailed particulars which were apt to change with time and circumstances. Unlike most of us, he was ever ready to confess his own errors—sometimes describing them as 'Himalayan blunders'. He laid no claim to infallibility, no claim to being a prophet. His highest aspiration was to be humble and sincere follower of truth which he identified with God. He reversed his earlier definition of God as truth to truth as God, on the plea that men sometimes disbelieve in God but no one dare disbelieve in truth.

I have referred to Gandhi's humanism. It was this that enabled him to make his apparently high-pitched, but deeply sincere, claim that his was an all inclusive love which left no one outside its circumference. 'Mine is not an exclusive love. I cannot love Muslims or Hindus and hate Englishmen. 'For, if I love Hindus and Muslims because their ways are, on the whole, pleasing to me, I shall soon begin to hate them when their ways displease me. A love that is based on the goodness of those whom you love, is a mercenary affair'. The reference to British people in this quotation is particularly revealing. As we all know, he suffered indignities and trials at the hands of the Government—particularly in the early years of the movement and spent about 3,400 days in Indian jails observing the jail discipline scrupulously and yet remained completely unembittered. He made it clear again and again that his quarrel was with the British Government and its policy of exploitation and denial of freedom to India. But not against the British people for whom he had great regard and respect:

> My attitude towards the English is one of utter friendliness and respect. I claim to be their friend because it is contrary to my nature to distrust a single human being or to believe that any nation on earth is incapable of redemption. I have respect for Englishmen because I recognize their bravery, their spirit of sacrifice for what they believe to be good for themselves, their cohesion and their power of vast organization.... I have hope of England because I have hope of India.... By a long course of prayerful discipline I have ceased for over 40 years to hate any body. But I can and do hate evil wherever it exists.... I hate the ruthless

> exploitation of India even as I hate, from the bottom of my heart, the hideous system of untouchability for which millions of Hindus have made themselves responsible. But I do not hate the domineering Englishman as I refuse to hate the domineering Hindus. I seek to reform them in all loving ways that are open to me. My non-cooperation has its roots not in hatred but in love.

This was a basic doctrine of his creed, which he upheld all his life:

> My love of the British is equal to that for my own people. I claim no merit for it, for I have equal love for all mankind, without exception. It demands no reciprocity. I own no enemy on earth. This is my creed.... I have known no distinction between relatives and strangers, countrymen and foreigners, white and coloured, Hindus and Indians of all other faiths, whether Muslims, Parsis, Christians or Jews.... I cannot claim this as a special virtue, as it is in my very nature, rather than a result of any effort on my part.

To a superficial student of Gandhiji's political career, it would appear that he was concerned only with India's freedom and not with wider international issues. But this is not correct. It is true that the international dimensions of India's foreign policy were spelt out by Pandit Nehru, but he was really developing what was implicit in Gandhiji's basic thought. 'My mission', he said, 'is not merely brotherhood of Indian humanity. My mission is not merely the freedom of India, though today it undoubtedly engrosses the whole of my life.... But, through the realization of the freedom of India, I hope to realize and carry on the mission of the brotherhood of man. There is no limit to extending our service to our neighbours across State-made frontiers'. For instance, it is well known that, before he was shot, he was planning to do in Pakistan what he had done in Bihar and Bengal—make a peace pilgrimage from village to village, trying to put down the flames of hatred and fanaticism. But, he said he could not do so effectively unless he had first extinguished these flames in India. He explained the relationship between the freedom of India and of the rest of the world in these lucid words:

> We want freedom for our country but not at the expense or exploitation of others, not so as to degrade other countries. I do not want the freedom of India, if it means the extinction or the disappearance of the Englishman. I want the freedom of my country so that other countries may learn some thing from my free country, so that the resources of my country might be utilized for the benefit of mankind.... My love, therefore, of nationalism or my idea of nationalism is that my country may become free, that, if need be, the whole country may die so that the human race may live. There is no room for race hatred here. Let this be our nationalism.

This was language which diplomacy had utterly forgotten to speak, an accent which had been a stranger to it! There was a unique quality of courage in Gandhiji's character. He feared neither the British Government, nor political parties, neither friends nor enemies, neither Indians nor foreigners. 'He who wrongs no one fears no one.' In his words, there is no bravery greater than a refusal to bend the knee to an earthly power, no matter how great and that without bitterness of spirit and in the fullness of faith that the spirit alone lives and nothing else does. With defiant courage, lie challenged the British Government: 'A Government that is evil has no room for good men and women except its prison. For me, the whole of India is a prison, even as the master's house is to his slave. A slave to be free must continuously rise against his slavery and be locked up in his master's cell for his rebellion. The cell door is the door to freedom'. When, in his famous trial at Ahmedabad he was charged with sedition and promoting disaffection against Government, he bluntly told the judge that 'dissatisfaction against such a Government is a virtue, for affection cannot be regulated or manipulated by law!' We are challenging the right of this Government 'because we consider its activity to be wholly evil. We want to overthrow the Government. We want to compel its submission to the people's will. We desire to show that the Government exists to serve the people, not the people to serve the Government. Whether we are one or many, we must refuse to purchase freedom at the cost of our cherished convictions'. He may well have pleaded justification for his actions in the words of an Arab poet who said: 'If the stand that I took was disobedience, then I desired by my disobedience obedience to God.' It was not only one man against the world but he made one feel that the world was in the dock and he was sitting in judgement on it. I have come across only one other example in our age of a person embodying in himself in the same way, the dignity of the whole of mankind—Bertrand Russell.

Gandhiji displayed this courage, his supreme fearlessness of all earthy power from the early years of his public life. It was evident not only in his fight with the British Government but also when he saw his own people and his followers going astray, which a rarer form of courage. In 1916 when he was a comparatively young man and not known all over India, he was invited to attend the opening ceremony of the Hindu University Central College. The meeting was presided over by Mrs. Annie Besant and attended by the Viceroy, the Governors, the Maharajas and Maharanis as well as some of the foremost leaders of the day. When he stood up to speak, he gently rebuked the glittering specimens assembled there, to flaunt their wealth and jewellery in a land of poverty and privation. This was a time when most persons did not even dare to open their mouth even in the presence of a British District Collector. In the face of the Chairman's discouragement and the walking out of some of the dignitaries from the meeting, he firmly pointed out, 'There is no salvation for India unless (among other things) you strip yourself of the jewellery and hold it in trust for your countrymen in India'.

Gandhiji had both the courage to give, when occasion demanded it, a fittingly crushing reply—albeit, in polite words and the grace to give the soft answer that 'turneth away wrath'.

I would like to share with you one example of each. The first is taken from a recently published book entitled 'Maharaja', for which Mrs. Naidu is quoted as an authority, I cannot, of course, vouch for its authenticity but it seems quite credible. On the occasion of the second Round Table Conference in London in 1931, Gandhiji was invited to the Royal reception at the Buckingham Palace. He attended it, dressed in his usual loin cloth—to the great consternation, incidentally, of many of the members of that sophisticated assembly. When he was introduced to King George V, who is reported to have looked excited and somewhat angry he told him: 'You were a friend of the British in Africa. I do not understand how you have now turned against me and the British Government. I warn you, if you create disturbance in India and do not cooperate with my Government, I have my army there to blow up all agitators and conspirators.' Gandhiji was too polite to enter into an argument at such a function and is reported to have remarked: 'I have not come to the party to discuss politics with the King,' But, a little while later, when he spoke at the final plenary session of the Conference, he referred to the talk he just had with 'an English gentlemen', not specifying him out of courtesy and simply observed: 'My children in India treat British bombs and bullets as mere crackers.' Obviously, the King did not know the mettle of the man with whom he had been talking—the fault not apparently his own but his adviser's. Addressing the delegates of the same Conference on another occasion, he said with supreme self-confidence and courage:

> Of course, the British Government may not tolerate, no Government has tolerated, open rebellion. No Government may tolerate civil disobedience (either...) I shall hope against hope, I shall strain every nerve to achieve an honourable settlement for my country, if I can do so without having to put the millions of my countrymen and women and even children, through this ordeal of fire. But (he added, speaking from a position of moral strength) if a further ordeal of fire has to be our lot, I shall approach it

with the greatest joy and the consolation that I was doing what I felt to be right, the country was doing what I felt to be right and the country will have the additional satisfaction of knowing that it was not at least taking lives but it was giving lives; it was not making the British people directly suffer, it was suffering (itself).... I do know that you will suffer, but I want you to suffer because I want to touch your hearts and, when your hearts have been touched, then will come the psychological moment for negotiations' (as it did come 14 years later).

Never was such language heard in a high political discussion, spoken with deep sincerity and readiness to match words with deeds. It must have made that assembly of seasoned and 'polished' statesman uncomfortable and ill at ease. But Gandhi could well have said with Plato: 'I would rather speak in my manner and die than speak in your manner and live'.

The example of the soft answer occurred when Churchill had made his well known statement that he had not become the King's first Minister in order to preside over the liquidation of the British Empire. He could not brook the idea of 'the half-naked fakir' walking up the steps of the Viceregal Palace, it seems to have shocked all his sense of propriety and of the social and political decorum for which, in his opinion, the Empire stood. Gandhiji read the statement and wrote this delightful letter to him. 'You are reported to have expressed the desire to crush 'the naked fakir', as you are said to have described me. I have been long trying to be a fakir and that naked—a more difficult task. I, therefore, regard the expression as a compliment, though unintended. I approach you then as such and ask you to trust and use me for the sake of your people and mine and through them of the whole world' and signed himself as your true friend, 'Gandhi'. Power drunk and contemptuous of the enslaved East and enslaved India as he was, Churchill never designed to reply and I do not suppose his 'wrath was turned'.

But time has sometimes its noble revenge. It must be said to the eternal credit of Gandhi, to the credit of his patience his goodwill and his technique or non-violence and also to the credit of the British people that, when it came to the parting of the ways, the traditions of Gandhi and Nehru made it, on the whole, a friendly parting. There had always been individual English men and women and small groups of dissenters who sided with the Indian freedom movement and stood out against the policies of their own Government. But the full miracle of reconciliation was seen only after Gandhi's death. In this year of his centenary, the British Parliament, representing the entire British people, has passed a unanimous resolution, placing on record their acknowledgement of his great work for the people of India and the world and of his friendship for the peoples of the U.K. 'That this House, on the occasion of the centenary year of Mahatma Gandhi, desire to place on record its acknowledgement of his great work for the people of this country, his life of simplicity and understanding which demonstrated to the world the importance of the brotherhood of man, the rejection of violence and the achievement of peace; and urges that strong support be given to the United Kingdom Committee responsible for celebrating the Gandhi Centenary in this country'.

It must, therefore, be admitted that, even in the present blood shot temper of the world, when some of the most cherished values of life are being defied and derided, good does sometimes triumph and vindicate itself, that it is possible to fight hate with love, darkness with light, ignorance with wisdom which is not knowledge but the grace of knowledge. The Nobel Prize Committee did not award him the prize for Peace—for political reasons, I suspect—but world public opinion has since conferred it on him several times over. To him, however, neither the denial nor the conferment meant anything. He was concerned with work not the 'kudos'.

I have given a few inadequate glimpses of the essentially loveable personality of Gandhi, which also highlight some facets of his greatness. But, if I may say so, the acid test of life is death. How does a man (or woman) face death—in fear and trembling like a coward or as one, who has fulfilled his mission in life as best as he could and welcomes death as a long lost friend who holds no terrors for him. One of our great Urdu poets, Iqbal, has described it as the gallant banner under which you can discover the true man of faith:

> Shall I tell you the true sign of a man of faith?
> When death comes, there is a (welcoming) smile on his lips!

Millions saw this smile of fulfilment and peace on the face of Gandhi in the calm of death as I saw it again, a few months back, on the face of another man of faith, Dr. Zakir Husain, as he passed away to meet his Maker. Gandhiji seemed to know that he, an apostle of non-violence, may be destined for a violent death. But he never showed any fear of it. Speaking a few weeks before his death, he had said: 'I don't want to die of a creeping paralysis of my faculties, a defeated man. An assassin's bullet may put an end to my life, I would welcome it. No one can escape death. Then why be afraid of it? It is my constant prayer that, even if I fall a victim to an assassin's buliet, I may deliver up my soul with the rememberance of God upon my lips. (And, then he added, with supreme, almost incredible self-confidence) I shall be content to be written clown as an imposter if my lips utter a word of anger or abuse against my assassin at the last moment.' He had also stated, at one of his prayer meetings, where a bomb was thrown at him, that he would deserve praise only if he fell as a result of such explosion and yet retained a smile on his face and no malice against the doer. He had added 'No one should look down upon the misguided youth who had thrown the bomb. He probably looks upon me as an enemy of Hinduism?. How nobly, how magnificently he passed this test, dying with the words 'Hai Ram' (Oh God) on his lips. He looked calmly unafraid into the bloodshot eyes of death and even death failed to quench the immortal spark of love compassion in his eyes. Of such stuff are true man of God made. Well may the Arab poet have said this of him, when he composed the couplet:

> You stood firm when there was no doubt that any one who stood must die—
> Stood, as though you were in the very eyelid of death and death was asleep.

I remember one of the characters in Shaw's 'Saint Joan' poignantly asking: 'Lord, when will thy world be safe for thy saints?' I could not answer this question on behalf of the Lord but I have the feeling that Gandhiji would have said: Only when it is safe and decent enough for the ordinary men and women to live in—men and women who are neither saints nor irredeemable sinners, in other words, common people who were his real constituency.

Gandhi was great in death as in life. He did many things, many great things. He gave back to his people their self-respect; he awakened the sleeping masses; he almost succeeded at one time in bridging the gulf between them and the classes; he raised the untouchables to the status of the Harijans; he championed the weak, the oppressed, the underprivileged, the women and the children, he won the political freedom of his country, using a unique weapon—the weapon of 'Ahimsa!' he tried to give social and economic content to this freedom; he defied the mad anger of the majority in order to protect the minorities; he rebuked the minorities when they appeared to be neglecting their role as free citizens of India and when the supreme testing moment came, he laid down his life with the name of God on his lips in order to make it possible for the Muslims to live honourably in the country. What a noble, what a tremendous achievement for a single life time!

Gandhiji had many great qualities but there was one supreme quality in him which was the inspiration for all the lovely things he did. This was the quality of his all embracing love and compassion (Karuna) which glowed like an incandescent light within the chandelier of his personality; love which is the primal emotion, breaking all man-made barriers, knocking down the walls of separatism enabling man to step beyond the boundaries of the ego and take the whole world to his bosom. Man, is like the resident of a lonely island, divided by deep seas from other men living on similar islands. Across these treacherous waters, he communicates with his fellow men through crude and still under-developed media of speech and signs. But love breaks through these barriers, making the whole world kin, casting out fear, enkindling hope and courage and compassion and cleansing selfishness and spite out of our system. Gandhiji believed that there could be no salvation for us as individuals, or for our crazy, hate filled world, unless love becomes a widespread inspiration. Love not as a superficial thing, not as an emotional or sensual indulgence, but in the deep and touching sense, as defined in the Psalms: And what a beautiful definition it 'is, its spirit often reflected in Gandhiji's own writings:

> Love is very patient, very kind. Love knows no jealousy, love makes no parade, gives itself no airs, love is never rude, never selfish, never irritated, never resentful. Love is never glad when others go wrong; love is gladdened by goodness, always slow to expose, always eager to believe the best, always hopeful, always patient. Love never disappoints.

Where I ask myself, has such love fled from this land of the great lovers of mankind? Echo repeats the question plaintively but answers not!

6

Quest for the Good Life

I must express my sincere thanks for the honour you have done me by inviting me to give the Bhatia Endowment Lectures for the year and also voice my high appreciation of the excellent work which this Institute has been doing so far as I have been able to judge in the field of culture and in fostering sanity of thinking in a world which seems inclined to turn away from it. Clarity of thought and decency of feeling are, after all, our only weapons of safety in this age, dominated by the menace of the atomic bomb, which is not only the name of a weapon of extraordinary destructiveness, but also a culminating symbol for a whole series of inhuman values and corruptions of thought developing over the centuries. Many years ago when the First World War was on and men were using what then looked like ultimate machines of horrible destruction, the editor of the *New Republic* of America wrote an editorial about the comparative power of bombs and creative human ideas, which I would like to share with you, because what was true in 1917 happens to be, alas, even truer in 1970, with some modifications.

> Who cares to paint a picture now, or to write any poetry or to search the meaning of language, or speculate about the constitution of matter? It seems like fiddling when Rome burns. Or to edit a magazine—to cover paper with ink, to care about hopes that have gone stale, to launch phrases that are lost in the uproar? What is the good now of thinking? What is a critic compared to a battalion of

infantry?.... Yet the fact remains that the final argument against cannon is ideas. The thoughts of men which seem so feeble are the only weapons they have against overwhelming force. It was a brain that conceived a gun, it was brains that organised the armies, it was the triumph of physics and chemistry that made possible the dreadnought. Men organised this superb destruction; they created this force, though it, dreamed it, planned it. It has got beyond their control. It has got into the service of hidden forces they do not understand. Men can master it only by clarifying their own will to end it, and making a civilization so thoroughly under their control that no machine can turn traitor to it. For while it takes as much skill to make a sword as a ploughshare, it takes a critical understanding of human values to prefer the ploughshare.... Knowing this, we cannot abandon the labour of thought. However crude and weak it may be, it is the only force that can pierce the accumulated passion and wrong-headedness of this disaster. We know how insecurely we have been living, how grudging, poor, mean, careless has been what we call civilization.... We shall not do better in the future by more stumbling and more panic. If our thought has been ineffective we shall not save ourselves by not thinking at all, for there is only one way to break the vicious circle of action, and that is by subjecting it endlessly to the most ruthless criticism of which we are capable.... The guilt for war comes home finally to all those who live carelessly, too lazy to think, too preoccupied to care, afraid to move, afraid to change, eager for a false peace, unwilling to pay the daily cost of sanity.

Those of us who work in the apparently unexciting world of ideas, who advocate good cause in speech and writing, trying to put them across to the new generation, sometimes tend to belittle their role and consider themselves of small significance in shaping the world of the future. I regard this modesty not only unjustified but, when it represents a collective reaction, almost criminal. It means they are giving up the fight even before it has been seriously joined: Bertrand Russell has spoken of the power of thought in words which deserve to become immortal and which form a worthy supplement to the editorial in the New Republic:

> Men fear thought as they fear nothing else on earth—more than ruin, more even than death. Thought is subversive and revolutionary, destructive and terrible; thought is merciless to privilege, established institutions and comfortable habits; thought is anarchic and lawless, indifferent of authority, careless of the well tried wisdom of the ages. Thought looks into the pit of hell and is not afraid. It sees man, a feeble speck, surrounded by unfathomable depths of silence; yet it bears itself proudly, as unmoved as if it were lord of the universe. Thought is great and swift and free, the light of the world and the chief glory of man.

When Madame Wadia graciously invited me to give these lectures, she indicated that their general theme was 'science and humanities'. This is certainly a very attractive field for speculation and exploration, but it put me into some difficulty also. It is a very vast field in which I had to find some pertinent point of reference from which I could start. In fact, on the face of it, they seem to be two fields, which for long have been regarded as almost mutually exclusive. I have no doubt many of you have read Edgar Snow's 'Two Cultures'—the culture of science and the culture of humanities which, according to him, have not been on speaking terms for a long time. I do not, however, agree with that postulate and will have to say something about it later. It occurred to me that perhaps a good theme might be 'The Quest for the Good Life.' It is a field which allows one a great deal or roaming space and, what is more important, both science and humanities have very significant contributions to make to the evolution of the good life. A good life which must base itself firmly on the fundamental values and the spirit of science as well as the insight, the vision and the social and moral values which the humanities can bring to bear on it.

Let me begin by pointing out that it would be wrong to assume, as has often been done in the past, that science is only concerned with the discovery of natural laws whose importance lies in the fact that, through them, we have been able to control the forces of nature and utilise them for our purposes. It is certainly *one* of its important functions, and it has made a remarkable contribution to the increase of man's productivity through the exploitation of his natural resources. If we compare what we can do in this field today with what we were able to do not only 200 or 400 years ago, but even 40 or 50 years ago, the progress seems incredible. Instead of travelling at a speed of say, 50 miles an hour, we can do so now at a speed of 20,000 miles an hour, with the result that man has almost beaten his own imagination and been able to set foot on the surface of the moon. It has certainly made the older dreams and imaginative visualizations of writers, poets and fable weavers about the moon outdated and revealed that it has a rocky soil, rather like the earth's and that it does not shine by its own light (as we knew earlier theoretically, thanks again to the insight of science). But while it may have deprived our poets of one source of fancy for their poetry—I say *may* have deprived, because I am not sure that they will give it up entirely as a challenge to their imagination—it has certainly opened up far greater sources of adventure and exploration. Or, I should rather say, it has opened up immense new possibilities in a field which has always been part of their literary heritage. That is the greater miracle of *man*—his mind, his creative imagination his powers of organisation, his response to the call of the universe which leads him on ceaselessly to find new domains to conquer. The poets can sing more exultantly of man, the conqueror of the moon and the stars. They have been doing so in a way from the dawn of civilization, when man had just learned to speak in graceful language and to think intelligently. In his *Antigone*, a tragedy of action, Sophocles sings a hymn neither to man's heroism, nor to the spirit of sacrifice shown by the heroine nor to the power of destiny but the object of his veneration is man's thinking *mind*:

> Language and thought, light and rapid as wind
> Man has taught himself these.

and it is through them that he can achieve or defeat his destiny.

Another equally remarkable contribution of science has been the speed and the facility with which not only goods and men but also their words, their idea, their discoveries can travel from one part of the globe to another, or even outside the globe. He can transmit electrical messages from the moon to the earth; he can flash across songs, speeches, photographs, news broadcasts in a way that practically annihilates distance. An epoch-making medical, or scientific, or technical or historical discovery can become the common property of mankind within hours. He is on the point of breaking the genetic code and perhaps discovering the secret of life which has been the most jealously guarded secret of nature. He has conquered most of the obstinate and intractable diseases which have dogged man's life through the ages—plague, cholera, smallpox, tuberculosis, yellow fever, and what not, though, it must be admitted, modern civilization has brought in its wake a whole host of new psycho-somatic and psychological diseases. With the help of science, we have doubled the average span of human life, considerably reduced the daily working hours in many parts of the world, enabled much larger numbers of people to enjoy poetry, painting and music and made the literature of the world more accessible to the common man. He has increased his capacity for making goods and articles of all kinds so enormously that they can pour out of factories and machines at his bidding in a veritable Niagara fall, as if at the waving of a magic wand. Whether this is good or bad or a mixed bag is a matter which we will discuss in due course. But there can be no doubt that man stands today in the full plenitude of his powers. Progress in the ordinary sense of the word does *not* now depend on chance—on some lucky discovery or invention—but is virtually at his command. He has at his disposal the tools with which he can fashion his destiny and he need no longer be at the mercy of the forces of nature and its unknown laws—at least in many aspects of his life.

The question, however, arises whether technology is the real end and fruit of science, whether it has done its job when it has enabled man to achieve these technological triumphs, whether new knowledge and insights, which science brings are only of value because they enable him to travel faster, to communicate better, to obtain freedom from hunger, ignorance and diseases and to live his every day material life more comfortably. These are all good things, I grant you, and neither you nor I would care to belittle their importance in the economy of life. And yet no great scientist or humanist, with a vision, will agree that this defines the full function and purpose of science in human life. It has many equally important, perhaps more important, benefits in its lap for mankind, if it has the vision and the perceptiveness to reach out for them. Science, in the first place, is the response of man to the ever new challenges of life; it satisfies his great urge to know, to explore, to discover, and to study and classify phenomena. Not because he may be able through these confrontations to make better cars or exploit mines or conquer other nations or destroy them more effectively, but because the quest for knowledge, the desire to open out new frontiers of thought satisfies one of the most fundamental cravings of his nature. A civilized man with an eager, creative, scientific mind cannot live with himself honourably, if he is unable to unravel the secrets of nature around him and is condemned to remain a prisoner of circumstances over which he has no control or in which he has no insight. No, in his magnificent audacity, he even challenges his Maker and pits his creativity against God Himself. In one of his short Persian poems, one of our great poets, Iqbal, has expressed, in the form of a dialogue, this creative tussle between God and man, each challenging the other.

Thou created the night, I the lamp;
Thou created the clay, I the vase!

Thou created jungles, mountains and deserts,
I created gardens, orchards and flower-plots!
It is I who make glass out of stone,
It is I who extract elixir out of poison.

So, the desire to know as well as the desire to achieve is inherent in the nature of man, and his self-fulfilment as a human being is impossible without it. This 'knowing' may or may not result in his doing something concrete or something immediately useful, but there is ineffable joy and self-expression in penetrating into the mysteries of the unknown and stepping into regions of thought, where no one has stepped before. When a mathematician made a great discovery, he was asked, 'What is the use of this discovery'? He replied, 'Thank God, there is none'. This is in some way the true spirit of science, though incidentally, this very discovery proved to be one of great practical utility at a later stage!

Again the adventure of science provides excellent discipline, not only in the field of the mind, but in the training of character and the nurturing of great values. Many persons, including some scientists' regard this activity as purely objective, as unrelated to character and irrelevant to the values which men and women of integrity have cherished through the ages and sought to encourage in their fellow men and women. Some scientists hold that they are only concerned with opening out new frontiers of thought and are neither interested in, nor responsible for, the consequences that may follow. I hold these assumptions to be unwarranted. Science is not only a body of knowledge but essentially a method of inquiry, and the use of this method calls for some values and qualities of character which have great social and moral significance. In the first place, science is the pursuit of scholarship, that is of truth, carried on by methods which have also to be rigorous, truthful and exact. In science you cannot achieve anything by cooking your results. You can deceive yourself and you may deceive others, but you cannot deceive science. You have to made absolutely sure of your facts and see that your conclusions are firmly based on them and not influenced by any prepossessions or prejudices. A scientist may develop a theory which seems to follow from a set of facts and honest observations. But he must test the theory at the anvil of practice. If he finds that, in a hundred instances, it works and in one it breaks down, he should have the courage and the integrity to discard or modify it or admit that he has failed for the moment. Integrity is, therefore, an essential part of a scientist's equipment—integrity of mind which is closely related to integrity of character.

Scientists are essentially a closely-knit *international* community. However great the distances that divide them, they must work co-operatively and carry on a mutually beneficial process of give-and-take. A scientist should also have confidence that his colleagues everywhere are dependable and ready to co-operate with fellow scientists everywhere. Science cannot progress if a scientist working, say, in the wilds of Africa cannot be sure that his colleagues working in Europe or China or Mexico will play fair with him and that they can all profit from one another's researches without being hoodwinked or let down.

These qualities—integrity, faith, independence, originality, capacity for dissent and objectivity—are not only fine intellectual qualities, but also the stuff out of which the fabric of the good life is woven. But I doubt whether, without careful effort, they are transferable to the social field. I do not wish to enter here into a discussion of the old controversy whether transfer of training does or does not take place form one field of activity to another and, if it dies, to what extent. There *have* been scientists, who allowed their standards of integrity to be corrupted by political considerations or observed them only in their narrow and specialised field. They did not carry them into the sphere of their social and political activities where, like many non-scientists, they let their narrow prejudices or irrational emotions run away with their judgement. This may be due to lack of adequate knowledge in these fields or the failure to made responses after carefully weighing the pros and cons, as they would have normally done in their scientific activity. But, whatever the cause, it does seem to suggest that a good scientist need not *necessarily* be a good citizen or a vessel of fine human values, though we must admit that some really great scientists have undoubtedly been both.

What is necessary, therefore—and this can be one of the great gifts of science—is to develop not only scientific knowledge and expertise and the methods of its practical application, but also the scientific *temper* and outlook, which will approach every problem from a genuinely scientific point of view *i.e.*, every problem where such an approach is relevant. What does it mean? Scientific temper involves, in the first place, an *objectivity of outlook* which refuses to allow truth, as it sees it, to be influenced by any other consideration—neither politics, nor religion, nor loyalty to the State nor the motive of making money. It is essentially a temper of *tolerance*, of readiness to entertain other ideas and points of view, of willingness to revise one's opinions if further evidence to the contrary, whether acquired personally or through others, becomes available. It never says 'My truth, right or wrong', but keeps its heart and mind open, knowing that truth is progressively revealed if honestly pursued, and no one has the right to think that he has achieved the absolute truth, which can never be challenged by men's advances in thought. It is also a temper which shows *reverence* and appreciation for those who have worked before, even though later researches and discoveries may have made them outdated. It is only over the shoulders of our predecessors that we have been able to catch fuller glimpses of our widening field. In many other important areas of human knowledge, it is not unusual to describe an earlier stage or phase of knowledge as obscurantist. In science, every true worker honours those who have gone before, marking precious milestones on the way. Newton does not cease to be a great scientist because Einstein has discovered new knowledge and postulated new theories in the field of physics. And he himself will continue to be a great name in the history of science, long after he has been surpassed by other researchers in the future. This respect for trail-blazers and for honest work is, therefore, an essential part of the scientific temper. It is a remarkable characteristic of the community of scientists, of the *true* scientists, that there are no barriers of caste or creed or sex or colour in it, that every one who is working in this field has free admittance to it and can express his mind freely, can contradict his colleagues and can be contradicted by them. The discoveries of scientists may become outdated, their theories proved incorrect, the new knowledge may contradict the old, but, as Bronowski has perceptively pointed out, 'Through all the changes of science, the society of scientists is flexible and single-minded together, and evolves and rights itself. In the language of science, it is a stable society'.

Then there is the important question of the social responsibility of the scientist for his work. There are some scientists who take a cold, almost inhuman view of their work. They would say 'we are only concerned with the progress of science and rest with its eventual consequences. It is for non-scientists—politicians, economists, industrialists, Governments—to make good or evil use of the power which science has placed at their disposal. We neither are, nor should be held responsible for what follows from, say, the invention of the internal combustion engine or splitting of the atom or the breeding of disease germs or of our work in various other fields. Now, this is an attitude which we, who are concerned with the welfare of mankind—whether scientists or humanists or social scientists—cannot possibly accept as sound and healthy. A person does not cease to be a socially responsible human being, whether he is a scientist, historian, philosopher, doctor or engineer. His sensitivity to social issues, to the impact of his intellectual or practical work on his fellow human beings is part of his human heritage which he cannot, and should not, barter away at any price. It is, however, a matter of satisfaction that some of the greatest scientists of the age have recognized the scientists' inalienable responsibility for the social consequences of their researches and discoveries. Many of the scientists *e.g.*, who were deeply involved in the splitting of the atom and the opening up of the possibility of making the nuclear bomb, like Einstein, Fermi, Oppenheimer made strong representations to the President of the United States against the decision to go ahead with the project of manufacturing it. But they were overruled. It would, therefore, not be quite fair to lay the blame for what happened exclusively on them. Politicians, military authorities, jingoists, who could see war only as the instrument of a competition in annihilation, turned a deaf ear to their advice, turned a blind eye to awful consequences that they knew would follow, let their hearts turn into stone, calcifying compassion with it, and rained death and destruction, misery and torture, on the civil population of Hiroshima and Nagasaki.

This should not, however, be understood as something that erupted suddenly, but only as the penultimate in cruelty and death-dealing. The process has been going on for centuries. Men have been tortured, burned, hanged, hacked to death, over the agonizing centuries and more recently, they have been subjected to the cruel refinement of bombing, poison gases, disease-germs etc. The nuclear bomb was, however, so much more powerful and destructive than all the other diabolical devices, designed earlier by man, that the difference in degree became a difference in kind. It shocked human conscience so powerfully that the Government of the United States spent—with mixed motives, no doubt—billions of dollars on the rehabilitation of Japan after its defeat, and sensitive individuals and organisations raised funds and tried to make honourable amends to some of the surviving victims of the tragedy. But man is, alas, a frighteningly adaptable animal. The shock passed away quickly enough and many persons learnt to take even these penultimates in disaster in their strides! And now, I understand, the hydrogen and cobalt bombs, which have been manufactured since, make the first two atom bombs seem like child's play. During this period of about twenty years, between the U.S.A. and the U.S.S.R. enough bombs have been stockpiled to make it possible for these two super-powers to wipe out the whole of mankind more than ten times over. Perhaps the naive questioner may ask: What is the fun in being able to kill dead persons over and over again? And if he really expects the policy-makers and war-mongers to give any rational reply, it will be further proof of his naivette. It was a Persian poet, who speaking of his beloved said:

Na mand kas ko ba tejh-i-nigah-i-naz kushi
Magar ke zindah kuni har kasay wa baz kushi

(No one is left whom you could kill with the arrows of your glances. Except that you bring them back to life and kill them again!)

So science is wrongly put in the dock and not the human monsters who have prostituted it to their unchaste and unholy purposes.

In spite of the incredible progress made by science and its handmaid technology, men have not yet grasped their significance in life. They do not realise that scientific method is even more important than the contents of science, that it can be used not only for the unravelling of the mysteries of the physical and biological universe, but also to some extent in the study of other disciplines which call for accuracy, objectivity, the adoption of research methods and development of high standards of scholarship. In addition, as I have pointed out, there are infinitely precious values associated with the pursuit of science which, if properly assimilated, *can* become part of the foundation, on which the good life can be built.

In the comparatively recent history of science, there was a period when people commonly believed that science and technology had changed or made obsolete the older values and beliefs on which the moral and social life of mankind has been built through the ages. There were many obvious contradictions between what men and women traditionally believed about the physical universe and the findings of the new knowledge discovered by science, between the superstitions and spurious miracles which had been woven into religious beliefs and the rational explanation of phenomena offered by science. It was, therefore assumed that men's motivations, the basis of their mutual relationships, the moral and social values which can give grace and dignity to life, must also be completely revolutionized, that none of the older traditions and insights, or few of them, had much relevance left for the modern age. I do not wish to deny the part truth that this view contains. It is a fact that changes in our life and conditions have exercised a very powerful influence on our ideas and patterns of behaviour and affected our social relations profoundly. If we fail to take them into account, we will not be able to live effectively and fruitfully in the modern world and face its new challenges. I have said, 'We should *take them into account,' not* accept or assimilate them *IN THEIR TOTALITY*. They may be welcome changes or harmful changes. It is part of man's great responsibility to use his discretion and wisdom in picking his way through this laybrinth. As the Quran puts it, 'We have shown man the way. It is now for him to be thankful or to reject God's guidance.' Nothing has happened in the last twenty or even two hundred years to negate the basic truth of what the great teachers of mankind have taught, since man acquired the rudiments of his moral consciousness. Many of the fundamental assumptions of human thought, on which a great deal of our social, moral and ethical philosophy is based, were worked out in the heyday of Greek civilization. Plato, Aristotle, Socrates etc., stand out not only as the earliest leaders of the world of the mind, but as thinkers whose significance even for our contemporary world remains unchallenged.

Our moral and spiritual development has been largely shaped by many persons of integrity and vision, who came in an unbroken sequences to invite people to the path of truth, justice and peace—prophets, saints, sages, seers, mystics and others—who gave life its spiritual dimension and filled it with moral content. It would be wrong to imagine that because man has split the atom or learnt to use electricity or to fly planes or to turn out products from the factories at a much greater speed, the whole moral heritage from the past has ceased to be of value.

In fact, technology can be a boon to mankind—and not a curse—only when it can be 'viewed humanistically', that is, made to serve ends which are primarily human and have to do, *not* with the production of material goods as such but, with enriching human life with significance and using these goods as a means towards that end. The *approach*, in my view, is even more important than the product. A country may want to exploit technology and increase its productivity for a variety of reasons. Its capitalists and industrialists or its government may want more wealth or power for themselves. Or its people may be mainly interested in raising their material standards of living, using more and more goods for the satisfaction of their increasing wants. Or, they may realise how most of their fellow human beings are being starved even of the bare necessities of everyday life and make an honest effort to ensure for them a decent modicum of living. Many other things, too, without which the good life cannot become a reality—education, health, reasonable housing facilities, leisure, opportunities fore recreation and cultural pursuits—cannot be provided unless the material substructure of the good life is well and truly laid. Thanks to technology, it has become possible for the first time in history, at least theoretically, to usher in an age of plenty for all, instead of an age of scarcity to which the majority of mankind has been condemned throughout history. But, so far, its increasing fruits have not been utilised wisely, justly and co-operatively, to make the good life possible for the common man. And, due to a variety or reasons, he is *not* prepared to accept tamely whatever miserable crumbs fall from the table of the rich and the well-to-do. He sees that some countries in the western world have actually entered the age of affluence, though not of social justice, with the result that this affluence is not equitably shared. In the U.S., for instance, society *as a whole* has been able to raise its standard of living quite high, though there are pockets of poverty and misery, which seem to make a mockery of the achievement. In his *The Affluent Society*, Professor Galbraith has developed the thesis that the Americans are not yet fully aware either of this fact or of its manifold consequences and obligations. While they often indulge in personal expenditure which can be described 'conspicuous waste', they have not yet realised how great are the resources they possess to devote to *public* expenditure which is good for the community as a whole and which can transform their whole pattern of life and thought—expenditure on child care, care of old people, education, housing, roads, hospitals, public health activities, opening of libraries, museums, art centres, etc. Not confined to show-places in urban areas but evenly spread out all over the country, with some preference to the needs of the long underprivileged areas. Many of these are no doubt, material things, but without their provision in reason, the good life for the common man cannot come into existence. Except for the comparatively small number of persons, who may choose the path of renunciation and seek, and succeed in finding, their satisfaction in a world which is furnished mainly with the furniture of the spirit—a world in which many men of God like Buddha, Jesus, Mohammad, St. Francis of Assisi, Gandhi, Vinoba, Schweitzer—have chosen to live. The physical benefits, which science has conferred upon us, have opened for many men, for the first time, the possibility of using their minds and spirit for creative, intellectual and artistic pursuits—their minds and spirits which had so far been chained not only by superstition, fear, religious bigotry and social tyranny, but also because they were living in a cramping economy of scarcity. Life, which had been limited for many centuries to back-breaking work which will just help to keep body and soul together, has now acquired potentially larger dimensions.

It should, however, be remembered that, with all the material furniture which I have mentioned, it is possible to miss out the good life altogether. When there is a confusion between means and ends, when man finds his mind clogged with earthly possessions, when the 'thing' kills the spirit, he can never go beyond it, like the common fly caught in honey. Side by side with his conquest of the world, man must develop his spirit of detachment which sees all the riches of the world lying at his feet, but is not ensnared by them and uses them not only for his own good but also the good of his fellow men and women. He should not allow the integrity of his mind and spirit to be polluted by them. Unless these things are done, the two-pillared good life, which neither rejects the world of matter nor the world of the spirit, but builds a bridge between them, cannot even make a start.

We have to remember that there is a certain deeply significant quality of mind which is both scientific and ethical, which does not judge things in terms of their utility or even in terms of what their reaction will be on other persons, but what it would be on the person himself. Any act, whether scientific or social, which degrades me as a person, which lessens my veracity or integrity, is a poor act, unworthy of the dignity of man. Bronowski has quoted two thought-provoking examples in his book *Science and the Human Values*, taken from the writings of the philosopher and mathematician W.K. Clifford, which bring out this point forcefully. They are a pointer to the good life at its *deepest* level, meaningful only for those who seek the real thing and are not anxious only to possess a make-believe, counterfeit article:

> If I steal money from any person, there may be no harm done by the mere transfer of possession, he may not feel the loss, or it may even prevent him from using the money badly. But I cannot help doing this great wrong towards Man, that I make myself dishonest. What hurts society is not that it should lose its property, but that it should become a den of thieves, for then it must cease to be society. This is why we ought not to do evil that good may come, for at any rate this great evil has come, that we have done evil and are made wicked thereby.

And what is true of an act of dishonesty at the social level is equally true of an act of dishonesty at the intellectual level.

In like manner, if I let myself believe anything on

insufficient evidence, there may be no great harm done by the mere belief; it may be true after all, or I may never have occasion to exhibit it in outward acts. But I cannot help doing this great wrong towards Man, that I make myself credulous. The danger to society is not merely that it should believe wrong things, though that is great enough; but that it should become credulous.

Let us then consider what exactly is the relationship between our progress in technology and our social, moral and ethical values. Are they unrelated, each free to go its own way, or are they so interdependent that every technological change necessarily alters the moral dimension of our lives and calls upon us to reshape our ethical thinking? The point is important because it is, to some extent, at the heart of the contemporary situation and quite different views have been taken in the matter. The orthodox communist doctrine is that social, moral and ethical concepts are largely the byproducts of the material conditions of life and reflect the dominant technological and economic patterns of contemporary society. There is also the opposite view that economics and technology do not matter profoundly, that moral laws are absolute and we must resist changes in them, if they are at all likely to come into conflict with our traditional moral values.

As is usually the case, both extreme views are untenable and it is necessary to located technology and ethics properly in the economy of human life. As I see it, technology attempts to alter the physical world in which we live, while our moral and social conscience concerns itself with ordering our personal and social relations. There is no *necessary* clash between them—the emphasis being on '*necessary*', for, in actual fact, there are often serious clashes between the demands they make on us. In the contemporary world, they cannot effectively and successfully fulfil their role unless these are resolved. By altering the properties of the stage, as it were, technology resets the problems which man has to face. But in so far as they are not purely technical or academic problems, their solution must be sought in the light of the general principles and ideals of conduct which a people may cherish. Viewed in this context, technology can only make good if it is pressed into the service of human needs, if it serves no *particular* class or group of persons but *man* as a whole, and takes a long range view, concerning itself both with the present and the future. Any attempt made, for instance, to exhaust ruthlessly and unwisely the precious treasures of the earth, unmindful of the future, is playing traitor to the welfare of the coming generations. Further, technology should be used wisely so as to make a contribution not only to man's *economic* well-being but, at least indirectly, to his *total* well-being, imaginatively viewed.

* * *

The good life has many faces and complexions and it would be wrong to try and envisage it, as if it were moulded in a single, unchanging pattern. It has to take into account the enormous variety of individual differences. This fact is known but not realised and appreciated enough and has not, therefore, been incorporated into the pattern of our thinking and behaviour. To take a trite but interesting example, I wonder how many of us have pondered over the fact that, of the billions of persons who live on this planet, no two are known to have identical thumb marks: If we visualise this fact of individual differences in the context of men's features, interests, aptitudes, intelligence quotients and social and emotional characteristics, how wide can their range be! It is, therefore, but natural that their mental equipment and qualities, their ways of self-expression and self-fulfilment, their concept of how they can achieve their own particular form and degree of excellence, should differ so greatly. The good life for 'A' cannot be a replica of the good life for 'B'. One may have artistic gifts and sensibilities, another may have academic and intellectual interests, a third may have practical gifts expressed in handicrafts, and a fourth may be a social type who can find his best expression in social service.

Psychologists have in fact, defined these various types, each with its own outstanding characteristics, and no one can achieve his maximum self-realisation except in his own particular line as marked by nature. It is, therefore, essential that our concept of the good life should be flexible, not rigid; tolerant not fanatical.

We must at the same time realise that there are some qualities which are almost universally necessary for the cultivation of the good life which should, broadly speaking, be manifested, in some degree, in *every* person who aspires after it. While these qualities have been variously described by different thinkers there is a basic unity beneath the diversity of their presentation. For instance, if one studies the writings of such different persons as John Dewey of America, Bertrand Russell of Great Britain and Tagore or Iqbal from India, one will find that they have all stressed in different ways the qualities of intelligence, courage and sensitivity as essential for the good life. Russell has specifically added to these the quality of *vitality* and Iqbal has mentioned the quality of *faqr*, which is, to some extent, a special contribution of Eastern thought.

Courage is regarded as an essential element in the good life—courage not merely as a negation of physical fear, but a positive quality, comprehending physical, intellectual and moral courage and the readiness to pay the price for one's convictions when they run contrary to what is generally accepted by one's society. It also involves the development of large, objective, impersonal interests, which give depth and breadth to personality and release it form bondage to fear, which usually dominates the life of selfish and self-centred egotists. Why? Mainly because they are afraid that, if their own little flame is extinguished, it will mean that the sun will go down on the universe! Not having developed any great interests and human concerns, in which they could lose themselves, they are always beset with various kinds of fears—fear of financial loss, fear of other persons who may do them harm, fear of illness, fear of death.

Courage also calls for the quality of genuine self-respect, which does not connote snobbishness or contempt of other, but is the fruit of the quiet conviction that, potentially, our individuality is infinitely precious, that we are gifted by nature with the inalienable right to think our own thoughts and do our own deeds on the basis of our first-hand experience, our knowledge and our individual sense of right and wrong. No one has the right to impose any unreasonable limitation on them. Anyone who surrenders this ultimate freedom for the sake of expediency or social approval can never attain the greatness of true courage. To him, Socrates will always be an inexplicable monomaniac, who foolishly preferred a cup of poison to the 'mere' renunciation of his true opinions. His thoughts and actions will be a pale and hesitant reflection of his particular society; he will never achieve emancipation from the dark kingdom of fear.

The second essential quality in this mosaic of the good life has been described as tolerance and compassion. It arises from what Russell has called social sensitivity, the ability to transcend the boundaries of our isolated ego and merge into the general stream of humanity. It enables one to share the joys and sorrows, the concerns and deprivations, the successes and failures of one's fellow men and women. Whether in the field of politics, religion, scientific thought or social life, it may be described as one of the kingpins of the good life. There can be no freedom, no rich variety in the patterns of culture, no appreciation of differences, no respect for the dignity of man, unless we actively cultivate this quality. It is a quality on which we used to pride ourselves in the past; we still do, only with far less justification—sometimes I have even the melancholy feeling that we do so with no justification at all!

I am averse in principle to trying to prove that the East is superior to the West, or vice versa; but latterly, a feeling has grown in the younger generation that we have had no great traditions of tolerance or charity in the past and have only borrowed it from the West. While no country or people has a clean escutcheon, it would be well to remember that we have had a far older tradition of tolerance than the West. I say so not to denigrate the West or boost the East, for I know that, in many things, it has surpassed us—for instance, in developing a superior and more comprehensive pattern of social services. But, if we are to avoid intolerance and fanaticism, we should see them as ugly excrescences on our culture, not as woven into its basic fabric. Also that it is only in recent centuries that the West has been able to eliminate from its life some of the most barbaric expressions of intolerance—though there have been from time to time, many frightful backslidings also as in Nazi Germany (but not only in Nazi Germany)....

The special contribution that the study of humanities can make to the moulding of a gracious pattern of life, is to create in students an awareness that we are all parts of one another, that the walls which usually divide us are artificial, that our basic unities are far more important than our separateness, that any indignity or damage or humiliation inflicted on any individual, wherever he may live, whatever his colour or race or sex or creed political beliefs, is an injury suffered by *me* personally, and it is part of my *dharma* to do whatever I can to resist it. As John Donne put it,

> No man is an island, entire of itself, every man is a piece of the continent, a part of the main; if a clod be washed away by the sea, Europe is it less, as well as if a promontory were, as well as if a manor of thy friends or of thine were; any man's death diminishes me, because I am involved in mankind; and therefore, never send or throw for when the bell tolls; it tolls for thee.

Literature, history, philosophy, arts and the social sciences can all reinforce this lesson in their own ways. They can do so provided they are presented by the right kind of persons and in the right spirit—teachers and others concerned with the shaping of our ideas and emotions who are themselves imbued with compassion and social sensitivity, and the institutions in the midst of which we live, provided they are humane, not exploitative. Otherwise, it is also possible to teach them in such a way that they make no creative impact but only cramp our emotions, strengthen our prejudices and poison our humanity. We have actually been experiencing this, to some extent, in the operation of our own educational system.

I have already referred to the supreme role of intelligence in life, in the context of the development of science and technology. This quality can, and should be developed, in the rich context of the humanities also. It would not be right to imaging that intelligence, which operates in the field of science, is quite different from that which expresses itself in the humanities. The scholarship needed in various humanistic disciplines calls for the same qualities of accuracy, honesty and objectivity of judgement. The difference arises partly from the fact that, in the case of the humanities, there are many more intangibles and variables involved, and, therefore, it is not possible to foresee consequences with the degree of accuracy which we can look forward to, when dealing with physical matter and physical laws. Even in the matter of physical laws, the earlier assumption that they were 100% accurate, that there were no exceptions, has given place to the theory that they are often in the nature of high approximations.

Secondly, in dealing with humanistic studies, we often go beyond the boundary of facts into the realm of values, where arriving at judgements is much more complicated and difficult and where great differences of opinion are possible and understandable. Einstein was once asked why it was that man has been able to make much greater progress in natural sciences than in the social sciences. His laconic answer was, 'Because the social sciences are much more difficult.' An answer that would surprise most persons, who believe that science and technology are complicated fields, meant only for specialists, while in problems concerned with sociology or education or morality or ethics or history of civilization or art and literature, any fool is qualified to express an opinion! The intelligence needed in this field has, however, to be tempered with humanism and wisdom. As one of our poets has said: 'Cultivate wisdom which has been schooled in reverence by the heart.' If intelligence is not thus tempered, if it does not become a tool for the achievement of social and humane purposes, for furthering justice, for fighting against the forces which have kept man in their thrall, denying him freedom of self-expression; if it is pressed into the service of exploitation, it cannot possibly become a part of the fabric of the good life.

This is really the great dichotomy from which man suffers—equipped with much greater knowledge and practical intelligence than ever before, but lacking in wisdom and the grace to use it for right ends. This was the lament made to the great Sufi poet, Rumi, by his Indian disciple, as expressed by Iqbal in one of his poems:

My thought scans the heavens,
While I live on earth in pain and degradation;
I am a failure in the affairs of the world,
Always stumbling blindly in this path!
Why am I unable to manage my business on earth?
Why is the wise man of religion a fool on earth!

Rumi cryptically replies,

He who can stalk across the skies,
Should not find it difficult to walk on earth.

This means that the claim to the possession of the powers of the spirit, including intelligence, is meaningless if it does not enable one to order the world of matter wisely and justly. These are not two entirely separate and different worlds but closely linked together by man's ambivalent life which is lived in both.

A special quality, which Iqbal has stressed and which does not usually find specific mention among Western writers, is that of *faqr*, a word which is rather difficult to translate or define in English. It does *not* mean mendicancy, as the derivative *faqir* as used in Urdu seems to imply. It is *not* renunciation because *faqr* does not call for a withdrawal from the world. It is really an attitude of mind, a spirit of detachment from the world which man retains even as he tries to conquer it; it is a refusal to be clogged by one's material possessions; it is the capacity to rise superior to them, realising that they are good if they feed the life of the spirit, but a dangerous snare when they push it into the background and themselves occupy the centre of the stage. It is a kind of intellectual and emotional asceticism, which does not need to turn away form the world as a source of evil or corruption, but uses it for the pursuit of worthy ends.

'In power as in subjection, *faqr* is the only shield which can protect the pure-hearted.'

The idea in stressing this quality as an essential ingredient of the good life is that, in the modern world which is dominantly and aggressively materialistic and where any other view of life has to be on the apologetic, 'things' will completely swamp man unless be cultivates this capacity for detachment.

I have come across another rather epigrammatic way of describing the qualities necessary to promote he good life. An English educationist described a truly educated man—not necessarily one who has graduated from a college or university but one whose *mind* is educated to face life with a reasonable chance of success—as one who can respond affirmatively to three questions.

First, can you entertain an idea? That is, have you an open mind which continues to grow and is ready to examine new ideas critically and without bias? Or have you a closed mind, to which things learnt in early life have become sacrosanct and which regards everything new with suspicion? Entertaining an idea does not necessarily mean accepting it, nor does it mean rejecting it outright. It calls for a readiness to examine it objectively, without any prejudice or prepossession or the complex of being omniscient.

Secondly, can you entertain the other fellow? That is, do you keep the windows of your heart open to the joys and sorrows of your fellow men and women, not regarding your petty ego as the most important thing in the universe? It is only when the drop becomes the ocean that it can acquire the power and majesty of the ocean. Otherwise, it is likely to be lost in the quicksands of self-centredness.

Thirdly, and this is in some ways even more difficult, can you entertain yourself? In the growing preoccupations and pressures of modern life, man is ceasing to be a friend to himself. He cannot carry on a meaningful dialogue with himself. He often finds his mind vacant and his thoughts, if any, boring. He fails to cultivate significant and worthy interests which might give some depth and meaning to his life and fill it, when the props of the routine activities of making a living have been withdrawn. He is, therefore, unable to make creative use of his leisure; he often does not know what to do with it at all and has often find silly time-killing activities. The Greek writer Epictetus has remarked:

> When you have shut your doors and darkened your room, remember never to say that you are alone, for you are not alone but God is within and your genius is within and what need have they of light to see what you are doing?

He was talking of his contemporaries, who perhaps had an inner life, who did not feel alone when they were alone, who did not find communion with self a boring experience. The plight of contemporary man, on the other hand is, summed up in this rather pathetic story. A man went to a doctor and complained that he was in the habit of talking to himself in sleep. The doctor remarked, 'Why do you worry about it? Many people are in the habit of doing so.' He replied, 'But doctor, your don't know, I am such a bore!' This is the difficulty that many of us face—we are such bores. Unless educated men and women have some deep cultural resources—and culture is more than superficial veneer on poor wood—there will be nothing that will stand them in good stead, when confronted by the trials of adversity or the temptations of prosperity, and they will continue to live their lives at a shallow level.

This stress on culture, I repeat, does not mean a belittling of the importance of its material infrastructure. The good life can neither be built on the foundations of materialism alone nor of idealism. Unless they are married together and the improvement of economic standards is made an object of urgency, so that people may be freed from poverty and starvation, all talk of culture and of spiritual riches will be meaningless.

But we must remember all the time that this is the beginning and not the end of the good life. While we should be duly cognizant of the material world, we should never forget or overlook man's spiritual world. The world of matter does not constitute the whole of reality and the cultured man cannot confine himself exclusively to its interests and problems. The goods of the mind, the riches of the spirit, the qualities that make for charity and humanism in social relations are too valuable to be sacrificed at the altar of crass materialism, as has often happened in affluent societies in different ages of history—from the time of the old Roman and Greek civilizations down to the present American civilization. Man's creativity is not confined to the reshaping of matter alone; he also has, in the forceful words of Iqbal, 'the capacity to build a much vaster world in the depths of his own inner being wherein he discovers sources of infinite joy and inspiration'—in art, in poetry, in literature, in science and philosophy and religion. In the pursuit of these cultural and spiritual goods, he should make use of the physical world as his raw material and exploit its possibilities for strengthening the upward movement of the human spirit. It is these that can provide the antidote to the boredom and the ennui which is the bane of modern life, even at its most affluent.

It is the combination of such qualities, in at least a modest measure, which can help and individual to move towards the goal of the good life. There are many other fine qualities which are necessary for persons who want to achieve success in special fields, like art or science or technology or medicine or public services. But if the object is to cultivate the great *art of living* as such, not efficiency in particular occupations or professions, these qualities, which have universal significance are necessary as a common denominator.

What is the difference, one may ask, between the roles of the sciences and the humanities in the repatterning of human life? I have already referred to the common features between them and that science is not unconcerned with human values. In fact, without some of these values, science cannot progress at all. One important difference is that humanities are not only descriptive and explanatory, but also normative. They tell us not only what happens or has happened, but also what should happen if the quality of life is to be enriched. The scientific value centre, as it were, round the stern values of truth. They do not include certain highly significant values like love, tenderness and compassion which give man's life its most distinctive quality. Men can become truly human—in the words of Norman Cousins—by cultivating 'a sense of beauty, a capacity to be enlarged by a tender experience and to be moved by compassionate thought'—qualities which are being crowded out of contemporary life by the increasing incidence of violence and the rejection of peace as a normal state of being. 'The mind of man is rapidly being hammered out of shape by the constant pounding of explosive accusations, denunciations and vilification—all tied to the casual and precipitate use of force.'

This is where, I suggest, the humanities have to meet the great challenge. If history and philosophy and poetry and literature and drama, cannot awaken in man a lively and practical response to the poignant human scene and some capacity to rise above the brute in himself, they have little value. But, in a world with rapidly changing contours, I am afraid our higher educational institutions have not yet realised the new challenging tasks that they have to face. They continue, as before, teaching un-lively materials and inert ideas and are unable either to make them relevant to the present situation or to work out their deeper ethical implications.

I disagree with those who hold that it is not the business of education to be concerned with values and ideals and that its real business is to impart knowledge and train intelligence. If this is a distrust of the didactic approach, I am one with them; for we know what the limitations of such an approach are and that it may sometimes act as a counter-suggestion. If, on the other hand, the idea is to limit the scope of education to the world of facts and to leave the realm of values out, it is crippling its effectiveness and denying its most exacting and rewarding responsibility. The study of the humanities should be able to illumine the deeper reaches of the human spirit and assess rightly the difference between what is good and what is evil. Bronowski has put it in words on which I cannot possibly improve: 'The values by which we are to survive are *not* rules for just and unjust conduct but are those deeper illuminations in whose light justice and injustice, good and evil, means and ends, are seen in fearful sharpness of outline.'

In spite of all that man has done to man in history, in spite of his having touched what the Quran has called *asfal-us-sefilin* (the lowest of the lowest depths), the unconquerable spirit of man, eager, creative, aspiring upward, has survived, and will survive all disasters. But for this faith, life will be a wholly unacceptable bargain. This is not merely my faith, which is perhaps of little significance, but the faith of many great and noble individuals who have touched life at its finest as well as life in the raw, who have enriched it generously, and fought valiantly against injustice, cruelty and heartless exploitation which corrupt its gracious promise. They have made an attempt to see man in the right focus and to distinguish between what is of permanent value and what represents vestiges of the long unhappy past and the bitter fruit of many new forces which have come into the ascendant, more aggressively, in recent decades—violence, greed, envy, the worship of the material and the neglect of what, for want of a better word, one can only call the spiritual.

To some extent, what man finds basic in life depends partly on the quality and nature of the person who is seeking and partly on what he wants to find. Miss Katherine Mayo came to India with a drain inspector's mentality, as someone called it. She found nothing except filth, misery and cruelty. They are certainly there, and I would be the last person to deny it. But there is much more in India, much finer things too that she was not able to see, because she had not the kind of eyes which could see beauty or gentleness. What is true of India is also true of other countries—they have their sunny side as well as their attractive side. I know of Indians who have been to the United States and were not able to see anything in it except sex and crime and the worship of wealth—neither democracy, nor philanthropy, nor evidence of generosity in personal relation-ships, not even the miracle of its great scientific progress. I know of some well known British historians who, after the First World War, wrote history books in which, it seems, they saw nothing in the German nation except what they called 'the eternal Germaniac' (This was the title of an actual book claiming to be an academic treatise written in the twenties). They were able to see in it only the faces of Bismarck, Hitler, Goebbels, Wagner, Schopenhauer who preached the message of death and not of Goethe, Lessing, Beethoven, Mendelssohn who preached the gospel of hope and the noble life. Again, there have been political commentators, economists, even men of letters, who saw in Soviet Russia only the pogroms, the liquidations, the suppression of individual freedom and the inhuman face of Stalin and neither the spectacular enlargement of the field of social services, nor the sharing of cultural and material riches more equitably nor the faces of Tolstoy, or Gorki or Turgeniev or Dostoevsky.... The point of my remark is that sweeping, uncharitable judgements of other peoples or of different groups in our own countries, based on the existing political and economic relationships between them or on racial prejudices, are unfair and unworthy and they tend to distort our whole view of life, our *weltanschauung*.

Yes, great is the spirit of man which has resisted injustice through the centuries and to which tributes have been paid by many discerning thinkers and men of vision. From amongst them, I would like to share with you the magnificent tribute paid by two of our great contemporary figures. The first is by Jawaharlal Nehru:

> I see in this past the long struggle of Man against adverse surroundings. I see his repeated martyrdom and crucifixion but I also see the spirit of man rising again and again and triumphing over every adversity. We may be a speck of dust on a soap bubble universe but that speck of dust contained something that was the mind and spirit of man. More wonderful than the earth and heavens is this spirit of man which grows ever mightier and seeks fresh worlds to conquer.... In spite of innumerable failings, man throughout the ages has sacrificed his life and all he held dear for an ideal—for truth, for faith, for country, for honour. That ideal may change but that capacity for self-sacrifice continues, and because of that much may be forgiven to man and it is impossible to lose hope for him. In the midst of disaster he has not lost his dignity or his faith in the values he cherished.

He knows that the future is dark and uncertain and yet his optimism cannot be defeated. 'We can see part of the way leading to it and can tread it with firm steps, remembering that nothing that can happen is likely to overcome the spirit of man which has survived so many perils. Remembering also that life for all its ills has joys and beauty, and we can always wander, if we know how to, in the enchanted woods of nature.

> What else is wisdom? What of man's endeavour
> Or God's high grace, so lovely and so great?
> To stand from fear set free, to breathe and wait;
> To hold a hand uplifted over Hate:

> And shall not Loveliness be loved for ever?

The other is by my favourite writer, Russell, who has always stood for the dignity of the human spirit and pleaded for it in words which will remain part of mankind's precious literary heritage:

> Brief and powerless is Man's life; on him and all his race the slow, sure doom falls pitiless and dark. Blind to good and evil, reckless of destruction, omnipotent matter rolls on its relentless way; for Man, condemned today to lose his dearest, tomorrow himself to pass through the gate of darkness, it remains only to cherish, as the blow falls, the lofty thoughts that ennoble his little day; disdaining the coward terrors of the slave of Fate, to worship at the shrine that his own hands have built; undismayed by the empire of chance, to preserve a mind, free from the wanton tyranny that rules his outward life; proudly defiant of the irresistible forces that tolerate, for a moment, his knowledge and his condemnation; to sustain alone, a weary but unyielding Atlas, the world that his own ideals have fashioned, despite the trampling march of unconscious power.

I see the quest of the good life then as an *open* possibility for man, which he may or may *not* be able to realise. It is neither barred out to him, as many pessimists and misanthropes believe, nor is it his for the asking, without the anguish and the ecstasy of hard, sustained effort and the faith which can strive against natural and human obstacles and against the gradient of man's folly and greed. In the words of Iqbal, which I quote from his famous lectures *On the Reconstruction of Religious Thought in Islam.*

> To the optimist Browning all is well with the world; to the pessimist Schopenhauer the world is one perpetual winter wherein a blind will expresses itself in a variety of living things which bemoan their existence for a moment and then disappear for ever.... The issue thus raised between

> optimism and pessimism cannot be finally decided at the present stage of our knowledge of the universe.... We cannot understand the full import of the great cosmic forces which work havoc and at the same time sustain and amplify life. The teaching of the Quran which believes in the possibility of improvement in the behaviour of man and his control over natural forces, is neither optimism nor pessimism. It is *meliorism* which recognises a growing Universe and is animated by the hope of man's eventual triumph over evil.

So, I present man to you as God's greatest miracle, greater than all the miracles mentioned in the scriptures of the world, greater than the miracles of science and technology, which he has himself created, greater than the miracles of art and beauty and thought which have poured out of his creative travail. In the trial of Joan of Arc, which Bernard Shaw has dramatised in his great drama, her inquisitors, imprisoned in their own blindness, are unable to reconcile themselves to her defiant thesis that man is a miracle, that freedom of thought and expression is a God-given gift which no church can take away from him, that even an irreligious or depraved person is sometimes capable of noble deeds. They cannot reconcile themselves to this heresy, and they resent her refusal to debase herself before the authority of the church, and so take their revenge, in the name of the Lord, by burning her at the stake, courageous and unrepentant! And yet, centuries later, truth triumphs like the bursting of a time bomb and the church is compelled to retrace its steps and to canonize her. Will you permit me to share with you the dialogue between Joan and her inquisitors, as interpreted by Shaw, because it throws significant light on what the good life means—at least in one of its many segments.

JOHN: I say that a true miracle is not done with a magic wand or incantation.... The true miracle is done by men themselves with the mind and the image that God has given to them.

BISHOP: You seem to be telling us quite calmly that God's true miracle is man, who is nothing but sin and error, blindness and futility—

JOHN: And strength too, and courage and light, sometimes when he is deepest in sin.

BISHOP: So then you excuse man all his faults and think him one of God's greatest miracles, even the only one?

JOAN: Yes, my Lord.

PROMOTER: It is blasphemy. Man is filth, lust, a nightmare of obscenity.

JOHN: Yes, my Lord. He sins, he is evil enough. And then something happens; it may be he is coming out of a brothel, roaring out his baudy songs in praise of a good time and, suddenly, he has thrown himself at the reins of a runaway horse to save some child he has never seen before; his bones are broken; he dies at peace.

PROMOTER: But he dies like an animal without a priest, in the full denomination of sin.

JOAN: No, my Lord. He dies in the light which was lighted within him when the world began. He behaved as a man both in doing evil and doing good and God created him in that contradiction to make his difficult way.

INQUISITOR: The enemy of the Inquisition is not the devil, the devil with the cloven hooves, the chastener of troublesome children. His only enemy is man—youth, generosity, human tenderness are names of the enemy. Man, calm and triumphant, frightens me infinitely more. Does he throw himself down supplicating God to hold him again by His hand? No, he turns away, suffers the torture, suffers humiliation and beating and replies: 'What I have done, I shall never wish to undo.' She will give you the same reply (to every question): 'What I have done, I have done. No one can make me disown it!'

JOAN: All that you can do is to kill me, to make me cry no matter what under torture, but make me say 'yes,' you cannot do. As long as one man remains who will not be broken, the *idea*, even if it dominates and pervades the rest of mankind, will not be in danger of perishing.

When man becomes identified, like Joan of Arc, with some great cause beyond himself and greater than himself, when his life's urges are expressed in some worthy, impersonal interests, he ceases to feel timid and insignificant because he knows that something in him will abide long after his own little candle has gone out—in the good that he is able to do to others, in the creative thinking of the world which he may have advanced or the contribution that he may have made to art or literature or culture. When this happens, the small drop becomes part of the great ocean, the mortal puts on the garb of immortality, and death ceases to have any terrors for him. This is the image of man questing for the good life, which I venture to place before you—man, the proud, the courageous, the compassionate, who will not lay down his arms before the cosmic forces of destruction and death but continue to light his lamp, though darkness may encompass the world. And was it not said a long time ago that all the darkness of the world cannot put out the light of a single candle?

So, the good life, as I see it, is a rainbow of many hues, some of which I have tried inadequately to analyse. It is *not* a straight line but a pattern which has depth and variety, which has basic colours, that I have specifically mentioned, and many other derivative colours which I have not. It is goodness and virtue; it is courage and independence; it is tenderness and compassion; it is response to beauty in all its infinite forms, in art, in literature, in music, in architecture, in men and women—not merely at the skin-deep level, but also as it shines out of a gracious face lined with wrinkles but illumined by an inner light. I cannot presume to describe it in words which can do justice to its fullness and will, therefore, content myself with giving you a noble passage from *The University Presbyterian*, which is entitled, 'Man Does Not Live by Bread Alone.' I have quoted it before, but it will bear repetition:

> Man does not live by bread alone, but by beauty and harmony, truth and goodness, work and recreation, affection and friendship, aspiration and worship.
>
> Not by bread alone, but by the splendour of the firmament at night, the glory of the heavens at dawn, the blending of colours at sunset, the loveliness of magnolia trees, the magnificence of mountains.
>
> Not by bread alone, but by the majesty of ocean breakers, the shimmer of moonlight on a calm lake, the flashing silver of a mountain torrent, the exquisite patterns of snow crystals, the creations of artists.
>
> Not by bread alone, but by the sweet song of a mocking-bird, the rustle of the wind in the trees, the magic of a violin, the sublimity of a softly lighted cathedral.
>
> Not by bread alone, but by the fragrance of roses, the scent of orange blossoms, the smell of new-mown hay, the clasp of a friend's hand, the tenderness of a mother's kiss.
>
> Not by bread alone, but by the lyrics of poets, the wisdom of sages, the holiness of saints, the biographies of great souls.
>
> Not by bread alone, but by comradeship and high adventure, seeking and finding, serving and sharing, loving and being loved.
>
> Man does not live by bread alone, but by being faithful in prayer, responding to the guidance of the Holy Spirit, finding and doing the loving will of God, now and eternally.

7

The Concept of Man

I have ventured to contribute this paper on the 'Concept of Man' to the Commemoration Volume which is being presented to Dr. Zakir Husain, partly because this theme is likely to be of interest to him and partly because, in his person, I have seen many vivid glimpses of the concept as I have tried to define it. It is comparatively easy to define a concept; it is much more difficult to *live* a concept, and this is precisely what he has been trying to do during his creative and fruitful three-score-and-ten years. The story of these years will, I hope, told by other contributors to the Volume. What I wish to point out, by way of a preamble to my contribution, is that Dr. Zakir Husain has been always greater than the exalted offices that he has been called upon to hold. He has added dignity to these offices, not shone in their reflected glory. This is not meant to belittle the importance of the offices. They *are* important because they give the individuals who hold them a greater and larger opportunity to make their impact. But if there is nothing significant in the persons concerned, no matter how extensive the screen in which they are projected, there would be hardly anything worthwhile to project. When Dr. Zakir Husain was a teacher in the Jamia Millia, then a very small institution in size, he was essentially the same person—with vision and imagination, with a luminous intellect and a compassionate heart, with unusual breadth of interests and sympathies and the capacity to see life and see it whole as when he was called upon to become the Vice-Chancellor of a University or the Governor of a State or the Vice-President of India. If tomorrow he were to become the Secretary-General of the United Nations or the President of India or, alternatively, to revert to teaching in a primary school or (God forbid) open a shop to sell cigarettes, the first alternative will not add anything to his human or intellectual stature, the second alternative will not take anything away from him. He will continue to be the universal man (as I have envisaged him), creative in his thinking and behaviour, sensitive to the finest values of art, literature, science, philosophy and religion. Such persons are the salt of the earth and there is no danger in his case of the salt losing, its savour. This is a tribute neither to the Vice-President, nor the Governor nor the Vice-Chancellor, nor even to the great educationist that he is, but a small tribute to the man whom I have had the privilege of knowing and assuming for a friend for many precious years.

II

There have been many, varied and often contradictory concepts of man, not only chronologically but also contemporaneously, and it is not possible to analyse them or sit in judgment on them in this short paper, even if I had the competence to do so. But many disturbing and interesting questions arise in my mind. Is man an accident or does he show some great design at work? Is he a creator or merely a creature entangled in the chains of *karma* or predetermination? Is he born essentially free and is everywhere in chains, as Rousseau claimed, or is he born with many chains and limitations from which he has to free himself by his own individual and cooperative efforts? Is he essentially good or essentially bad? And, remember, both claims have been made by schools of thought which we cannot possibly ignore. Is pessimism the right approach for man or optimism or, what

Iqbal has called, meliorism which means the potentiality to improve continuously? Is he to find his salvation and fulifilment in becoming a passive tool of society and move towards the ideal of the 'organisation man' or does he come into his own by developing a strong and unique individuality which can, when the occasion arises, defy society and stand as one man against the world? Was Hitler in his view of man as a tool of the State or the many men of God who looked upon him as an entity of infinite value, with a spark of the divine in him? Is he immortal or is he a candidate for immortality who can achieve it but may not, if he does not develop, the requisite qualities? Is man essentially a physico-chemical organism or a psycho-physical organism or a vessel which contains the Holy grail? Is he a matter or spirit or a combination of both, and is this combination a 'physical' mixture or a chemical compound transcending both? Again, is man basically the communal, the racial, the geographical, the linguistic, the national man or is he the universal man on the way to becoming one? Is diversity his characteristic quality or unity? Should he be regarded as the centre of the cosmos, as he has been fondly imagining himself, since the power of abstract thinking emerged in him, or as an infinitely small organism on an insignificant speck of dust? The earth itself has been now relegated, by modern astronomical discoveries, to the position of a second rate planet attached to a second rate sun, floating helplessly in the endless cosmos. And just as astronomy has given us a sense of geographical infinity, so has biology given us a sense of the temporal infinity of the universe. In these new dimensions, what is the real significance of this 5 to 6 ft. tall biped? Can we reasonably continue to have the flattering image of our species which has haunted our dreams and imagination—man as Nature's magnum opus, as the Lord of the universe, as the Vicegerant of God on earth, as the end of all creation? Again, which is the real Man—man who has been a literal or figurative cannibal throughout history, who has carried on innumerable wars of destruction and killing of his own species, who inflicted even on his coreligionists the tortures of the Spanish Inquisition, who (in the course of history) has perpetrated inhuman cruelties on the depressed classes in India, the Negroes in America and tile South African blacks, who has exterminated six million Jews with incredible sophistication of torture, who has carried out bloody purges in U.S.S.R. and China, who dropped the atom bombs in Japan and who is still thoughtlessly designing bombs of infinitely greater destructive power, with the ambition of acquiring the capacity to overkill mankind ten or twenty times over, who (even when he is not indulging in these spectacular acts of inhumanity) is content to see the bulk of his species live less than human lives without his days and nights being made hell for him, who adds treachery and deceipt to all the other cruelties which even the so-called lower animals do not do. Is this the real Man or one who preferred to drink poison rather than renounce his right to the pursuit of truth and one who renounced the kingdom of this world to preach the gospel of compassion, or one who climbed the cross with a view to establish the kingdom of God on earth, or one who spent his life, in spite of every possible discouragement and mistreatment, teaching the gospel of human fraternity without distinction of caste, creed or colour, or one who renounced the life of a great artist to work as a doctor in the wilds of Africa or one who walked bare-footed in the villages to put out the flames of hatred and welcomed the murderer's bullet with 'Hai Ram' on smiling, lips, or one who has the hardihood to go and deliberately expose himself to bombing in an area with which he has no religious or racial or geographical affinity? So many questions arise in the mind that I could exhaust all the time at my disposal and more—asking them and thus need not answer any of them.

Let me, however, try to elucidate briefly, a few of these as I see them. I realize, however, that in defining what this concept *is*, there is a danger that one may also, consciously or unconsciously, define what one considers this concept *should* be. This is not, however, altogether an unwelcome risk. Firstly, these questions indicate that we should not try to find any glib, universal answers which will be applicable to all. Man is not this or that. Man is this as well as that and many more things than we know of. All these different types, envisaged in the rhetorical questions that I have ventured to ask, are men—the good, the bad, the indifferent, the cruel, the compassionate, the mechanical, the creative, the myopic, the visionary—representing the different facets of the species Man. We cannot ignore any of them; we cannot shut the doors of our heart to them. We have to hate and condemn the sin and the crime but—difficult as it is to say so—not the sinner and the criminal; for there, but for grace of God, go you or I! We are enjoined by all that is good and worthy in our spiritual heritage to endeavour, slowly but persistently, to move from the first category of haters and wrong doers towards the second category of men who have charity and compassion and a sense of beauty and goodness, in whom mankind finds its finest apotheosis. And we have to labour ceaselessly to create the conditions in which this miracle may be possible—not with any miraculous speed for that is a miracle which never happens—so that slowly these qualities may begin to have an edge, in the lives of an increasing number of men and women, over cruelty, injustice, exploitation and social artistic insensitiveness. In other words, we cannot be content with, Saint Joan's agonised question in Shaw's play: 'O God, that madest this beautiful world, when will it ready to receive the saints?' It is not God who has taken upon Himself the responsibility of making it ready for the purpose. He has—for those who believe in Him—entrusted this responsibility to Man. And for those who do not believe in God, the responsibility is still Man's whether placed on him by Nature or his own conscience. Nor one may add parenthetically, can it really be called a 'beautiful world'—in spite of all the innumerable and breathtaking beauties it has—unless it has been made fit not only to receive His saints but also to harbour its ordinary men and women and provide for them the possibility to lead peaceful, constructive and happy lives. So one may perhaps hazard the opinion that there is justification neither for pessimism on our part, which condemns everyone but ourselves, nor for that easy, effortless, comfortable optimism which does not even recognize the need for any effort on man's part to improve the world in which he is living. If the world is to be 'filled with justice and truth', as the Quranic phrase goes, he has to take an active part in the process, buoyed up with the hope that he will eventually triumph over evil and injustice, that he has made over the centuries marvellous conquests in the realm of the matter, the mind and the spirit—and has yet to make many more, that as he has been able to control the tyrannies of Nature over man, he will also be able to defeat the tyrannies of man over man which are even more obstinate and deep-rooted. These were due, at least in part, to the fact that in the past, man had to contend with his brother man ruthlessly in order to win some security for himself in an economy of persistent scarcity. And the good things of life went to him who was physically stronger or more wily and treacherous and could exploit others for his own personal or group benefit. But modern science and technology have at least opened out the possibility of ensuring an economy of plenty for all—provided, amongst other things, increase in population can be controlled. If men and nations could live without their actions being governed by a blind, snatch-and-grab policy, one great source of conflict would be removed and they could lead more rational, peaceful and kindly lives.

This brings into focus a controversy about the concept of man which has been with us for a long, long time. What is *the essential* nature of man's life' Is it primarily material or spiritual? If it is both, which one takes priority over the other? The difficulty is that, if one stresses the material aspect as important, one is accused of being materialistic and insensitive to higher values. If one stresses, the spiritual, one is accused of running away from reality, of not recognising the facts of life, of living in an unreal dream world. The truth is really obscured by this either-or approach. Man is the end product of a process of biological evolution which is millions of years old; he has a physical body with its creature needs and urges and, if they are not adequately satisfied, he suffers, he is frustrated, he fights and is, generally speaking, unable to appreciate the higher things which life can bring. On the other hand, if the multiplication and satisfaction of creature needs is all that matters, if he lives by bread alone in what way is he superior or more worthwhile than the innumerable other creatures who are also interested in the same thing, though their needs are more limited and their built-in devices for meeting them more perfect? To the best of our knowledge, man is the only sentient creature in the universe in whose case evolution has taken, as it were, a new mutation, equipping him with a mind which can reflect, with the power of speech which makes intelligent and intelligible communication with other men possible and with the capacity to progress indefinitely and conquer new realms of meaning and new domains of beauty. No one can explain why only on this little earth, this great miracle should have taken place while the rest of the planets and stars should, so far as we know, lie dark, uninhabited, unillumined by intelligence. I need not discuss here the great and creative role that the mind has played in his evolution, having attempted to do so in a recent book of mine,[1] but would only point out that it has given to his life vast and entirely new dimension with which we must reckon. He cannot obviously rest content with merely conquering the world of matter, but must also wrestle with the world of the spirit and grow into wisdom, charity and sense of beauty, and cultivate wide and varied interests in which his personality may find its richness and fulfilment. In the words of Percy Nunn, 'this higher creative life, far from being an accident, is the clearest and purest expression of the essential characteristic of life at *all* its points and levels. All life, however humdrum, is permeated, by the self-same-element whose inflorescence is literature, art, philosophy, science and religion.'

It follows, therefore, that any concept of man which ignores or belittles these values is essentially wrong and incomplete. The conflict of views, of course, is seldom posited in terms of stark contrasts, but the difference of emphasis is often strong enough to make it almost a difference of kind. The changes, that have come in the wake of man's scientific, industries and technological progress, have tended to place increasing emphasis on material values, while those who uphold spiritual values have been driven more and more to the defensive. The political and economic supremacy of Western Europe and America, their success is moving towards an affluent society have given them a new prestige and other countries have tended or aspired to follow them. While it must be acknowledged that some of their finest minds and most sensitive spirits are deeply concerned and anxious about their existing situation, and various schools of philosophical and ethical thought contend for supremacy, it seems that a materialistic view of life and of man is actually in the ascendent. Bertrand Russell has sounded a note of alarm against this danger in unmistakable terms. 'Man's true life does not consist in the business of filling his belly and clothing his body but in art and thought and love, in the creation of beauty and in the scientific understanding of the world.'

It would be well to recall that, traditionally, India and the East have stood for values other than material, and their best thinkers have acknowledged their superior importance. Their weakness has often been that they have tended to ignore the misery, the squalor, the ignorance in which the masses lived and sought refuge in the ivory tower of these values and cultivated them outside their social milieu. While rectifying this mistake, it is necessary to reaffirm their primacy emphatically. I would even venture to say that there is a great deal to be said for what may be described as a tempered ascetic approach to life, provided asceticism is not for the other fellow but for oneself, where compassion for the suffering of other and effort to ease it is combined with a sense of detachment and a capacity to reject the temptations of the world so far as one's own attitude to life is concerned. Mahatma Gandhi in our own days has been the unapologetic protagonist of this view. 'In so far as we have made the modern materialistic craze our goal, so far are we going downhill in the path of progress. That you cannot serve God and mammon is an economic truth of the highest value. Let us first seek the kingdom of God and His righteousness and the irrevocable promise is that everything will be added unto us'. And, conscious of the fact that many hard-headed realists will dismiss this as impracticable idealism, he adds: 'We need not be afraid of ideas or of reducing them to practice even to the uttermost. Ours will only then be a truly spiritual nation when we shall show more truth than gold, greater fearlessness then pomp of pride and wealth, greater charity than love of self'.

This is not, however, an isolated voice. It is woven not only in our historic traditions of philosophical thought but inspires the thinking of many of our best contemporary thinkers also. Let me give a few examples. Nehru, who was cast in a different ideological mould, was also keenly sensitive to this issue. 'The passion for riches, for acquisition, for more and more wealth tends to create jealousies and conflicts. If the objective aimed at is social balance in a community or the world at large, production by itself does not achieve it. Indeed, it tends to create greater imbalance... Too much wealth and affluence, whether in an individual or a society has also its attendant evils which are becoming evident today. The mere piling up of material riches may lead to an emptiness in the inner life of a man'. Iqbal who has interpreted the teaching of Islam in this context brilliantly in his Lectures on the Reconstruction of Religious Thought in Islam, advocated that we should confidently say 'yes' to the world of matter but never forget that primacy belongs to the spirit, that while, in the early stages of evolution, the mental is dominated by the physical, as it grows in power, it tends to dominate the physical. This is how he elucidates his view of man and life:

The ultimate reality, according to Quran, is spiritual and its life consists in its temporal activity. The spirit finds its opportunity in the natural, the material and the secular. All that is secular is, therefore, sacred in the roots of its being. The greatest service that modern thought has rendered to Islam and, as a matter of fact, to all religions, consists in its criticism of what we call material or natural—a criticism which discloses that the material has no substance unless we discover in the spiritual. There is no such thing as a profane world. All this immensity of matter constitutes a scope for the self-realization of the spirit. As the Prophet so beautifully puts it: 'The whole of this earth is a mosque.'

Tagore, similarly, highlighted the importance of developing the inner resources of the spirit which lie embedded in every individual, provided he does not let them become atrophied by what he called the 'Thing', i.e. the blind accumulation of material goods and riches. The claim sometimes made by the eastern nations that they are superior to the west on the basis of an alleged, rootless spirituality is as untenable as the counter-claim by the West that it is superior to the East because it has better plumbing or because it can manufacture the atom bomb! It is here and now that men and women must learn to live justly and cultivate their inner spiritual resources so as to give direction and meaning to their daily life.

Azad has pointed out, in his Presidential Address at a Unesco seminar on Humanism in East & West, that in Indian thought the point of emphasis has always been the inner experience of man and, in this search, it has ventured to penetrate below the regions of sense and intellect and 'sought to assert the identity of man with a deep hidden Reality'. According to Sufi and Vedantic thought, man is not a material entity only; he is variously described as an 'incarnation of God', 'the highest manifestation of God's being', 'a wave of the boundless sea', 'a ray of the sun that is God', 'a movement in the being of the Eternal'.

To Radhakrishnan, man is not merely a biological or economic being but also a spirit. Power and wealth, with all their arrogance, their common acceptance as the current coin and their tight hold on the minds of men, are shadows that pass; what abides are qualities of compassion for the weak, faith in the unity of mankind, irrespective of the distinctions of race, caste, creed or colour, devotion to the ideals of peace and freedom and sensitiveness to beauty in all its forms and manifestations. According to the fundamental outlook, which has dominated the spiritual landscape of the country, 'he who, by the power of his meditation, establishes supremacy over his appetite and emotions, is greater than one who is able to win the battles of the world; in other words, self conquest is more important than conquest of countries.' An Iranian poet expressed the same view in the words: 'To fly in the air is no miracle, for the dirtiest of flies can do so; to cross rivers without bridges or boats is no miracle for a terrier can do the same. But to help the suffering hearts is a miracle only performed by holy men.'

This discussion of the place of the material and the spiritual in the concept of man also throws some light on one of the numerous question which I raised at the outset. Man, as we see him in this mirror, is not essentially translatable in racial, geographical, communal, or linguistic terms. These are certainly facts which have to be taken into account and due allowance made for them but they have a limited significance—they do not represent the ultimate reality. When we are content to define a man as a negro, or as a Hindu or a communist or Arabic-speaking, we may be referring to a facet of his personality or an accident of his birth—we are *not* encompassing him as a whole. Man, in his essence, transcends and should learn to transcend these limitations—not, indeed, in the, sense of ignoring them but of being able to rise above them—and view himself as a part of the whole of mankind. 'I sometimes think,' mused Azad in one of his speeches, 'that it was better when men and women believed implicity in the story of the Bible and thought that, whatever be the differences between nations and races, they were all the children of Adam and Eve. In the 19th century, as our knowledge increased, we started questioning these religious legends. Instead of believing in descent, from common parents, we started to divide mankind into Caucasians and Mongolians, into Aryans and Semetics and into further subdivisions within each larger division. I do not know if the story of Adam and Eve is *literally* true, but I have no doubt that it is true in essence; it is a recognition of the fundamental truth that the human race is one in origin and hence all men are akin to one another.' Such divisions are actually methods of classification, distinctions of convenience. In the words of the Prophet of Islam 'The whole of mankind is the family of God' and, according to the Quran, 'We divided you into tribes and classes so that you may be known.' But the *means*, have often been confused by short-sighted man with *ends*, and he has learnt to view himself as irrevocably divided into narrow categories. He looked upon his fellow men and women as 'competitors or rivals or obstacles to his own advance', and not as 'co-hairs of the grace of life, as fellow members of (a common) spiritual household'. This has always been a moral and social tragedy and a denial of his true nature. But in this one world of today, it is a danger and disaster of unimaginable magnitude. We must either gradually reduce it and eventually eliminate it or, with the atomic threat hanging over our head, there may not even be persons left to carry on this Great Debate; Mankind can realize this unity only by developing a world perspective in which the ideas and ideals of different civilization and culture are properly assessed and harmonized and treated with objectivity and without prejudice'.

I have so far referred, mainly to two important elements that enter into the concept of man—the relationship of the material and the spiritual in him and his universality rather than division into categories. But its most distinguishing characteristic, as I see it, which marks him out from other creatures sharply is his *creativity.* He is referred to in the scriptures as 'made in the image of God'—if so, it must be in the image of God, the creator. It is interesting to note that most of the non-human creatures are superior to man either in size of strength or speed or endurance or the capacity to defend themselves and to find their food and build their nests or other habitations by instinct. If the Creator had not conferred on man the gift of potential creativity, he could hardly have competed against them with any measure of success. He has, therefore, to cherish and cultivate this gift with great care and use it to offset all the disadvantages from which he suffers and, to the extent that he has been able to do so, he has scored over them and achieved his greatest triumphs. They are great, indeed, though uneven in different fields. But compared to what he can and has still to do, they are not morel than the portion of a glacier visible above the waters. In his inmost being, man is a creative activity shaping his destiny and that of the world in which he lives, sometimes moulding them to his own purposes, sometimes adjusting himself to its forces. But he is creative also in the deeper sense; he is not helplessly imprisoned in this world which surrounds him. When he is thwarted by its forces, he has the capacity to build a much vaster world in the depth of his own being, wherein he discovers sources of infinite joy and inspiration. In the words of Iqbal, 'Hard his lot and frail his being like a rose leaf, yet no form of reality is so powerful, so inspiring and so beautiful as the spirit of man'. This is the world of art and letters, music and painting, philosophy and science in which his mind and heart, the sources, of his creativity, find their highest expression and fulfilment. He does not—or should not—indeed create it in order to find an alternative world in which, he may, take refuge from this vale of sorrows but with the object of transforming it into a worthy habitation for himself and his fellow men. All the material riches, the power, the knowledge that he has acquired are not the end but, at best, the starting point of his great spiritual quest. At their worst, they can kill that quest by diverting his attention and loyalties to lesser objectives.

Not only does man play creative role in this world but the world itself is, in a process of 'becoming'—it is an 'expanding world' as James Jeans and many other distinguished scientist are beginning, to interpret it. And this goes on sharpening and re-defining the challenges which man's mind has to face. 'To my mind', Iqbal points out, 'there is nothing more alien to the Quranic world than the idea that the universe is the temporal working out of a preconceived plan. The universe, according to the Quran, is liable to increase. It is a *growing* universe and *not* an already completed product which left the hands of its Maker ages ago and is now lying stretched in space as a dead mass of matter to which time does nothing and consequently is nothing'. If, on the other hand, it were regarded as a process realizing a preordained goal, there would be no room in it for free responsible moral agents'. It would be but 'a stage on which puppets are made to move by a kind of pull from without'. No, man s creative mind is perpetually active—sometimes constructively, sometimes destructively and, picturesque words of Whitehead, 'our minds build cathedrals before the workmen have moved a stone and our minds destroy them before the elements have worn out their arches'. Modern men must, therefore, learn to prepare himself for a world of 'plural possibilities' where he has not only to make right choices but also to train his mind and creative intelligence in such a way that he may be able to tackle new jobs and meet the challenge of new problems both in the world of thought and action. This has always been, in a way, man's responsibility, but in the past it was often performed by a very small minority, while the majority was chained to the tread-mill of earning a scanty living and unable to play a creative role. Now, in spite of the fact that there are many contrary forces that one must recognize, the challenge comes to all of us, and refusal to face it is refusal to recognize man's freedom and dignity.

There is a tendency in the present age to belittle the role

and importance of the creative individual and to submerge him in the mass. This is partly a bye-product of the industrial and technological revolutions, of the emergence of the big businesses and of the impact on society of totalitarianism, capitalism, and socialism, though their protagonists may not admit it. This view of the role of the individual in society is both wrong and immoral. The individual *is* frightfully important—nothing either good or bad can really enter the world except through his free activities. The mass can never compensate for the quality and uniqueness that belongs to him. Man has become, to a considerable extent, the director of his own evolutionary process, which is now social and cultural rather than biological, and this poses problems that only a creative mind can deal with intelligently. Such minds are needed not merely to solve academic, intellectual and scientific problems through research—that is obvious enough—but, even more so, the new and challenging problems that are arising in the field of social and political relationships, in the domain of ethics and morality which are even more exacting. Sometimes a single, creative individual can make a greater impact on the life of his country or his age than millions of mediocrities put together. To take two entirely different kinds of examples—an Einstein or a Gandhi has really far greater ultimate significance for the human race than any number of good, decent, socially worthy but humdrum individuals. One important function of such unique individuals is to act as dissenters against society when the occasion demands it, for that is the only way in which we can reappraise and re-assess the values by which society gets used to living without raising any questions. They must do so with supreme concern for what they consider to be the truth and supreme unconcern for everything that comes in the way.

And yet the creative individual cannot flourish in isolation. The individual and the society are both involved in the process. The 'potentially creative' minority in a society can never become an effective one, unless its spiritual and intellectual climate is favourable to its growth and the people have the vision, the good sense and the tolerance to welcome and appreciate such persons. I know that there are geniuses whom nothing can repress, but they must be regarded as exceptions. We have no idea of how much of first class talent is killed by indifference or by the failure to provide the conditions in which it can freely develop. Freedom itself is the first and foremost of these conditions, for creativity cannot move along predetermined grooves. In fact, it is creativity just because it rejects them and blazes its own new and unexpected trail. Arnold Toynbee has pointed out two obstacles which hinder its development. First, the ultra—egalitarianism of democracy which looks askance at any unusual evidence of talent and considers encouragement of meritocracy as a kind of at least minor crime against it—as if democracy meant 'the equal assessment of unequal merit'. In such a society 'toleration is the alluring reward of poor spirited conformity'. So, many highly promising children and youth, gifted with genius, who are unable to face expressed, or unexpressed hostile public opinion, choose the path of least resistance and let their talents wither. This has been happening not only in our country and other educationally backward countries but even in many advanced countries of western Europe and America. The other hindrance is the deep-rooted conservatism in many societies which is averse to change and wishes to maintain the status quo, largely in favour of vested interests. Creativity, on the other hand, is a factor of change; it upsets the established order in answer to new challenges. It is opposed by some because it threatens their undeserved, unearnt privileges and by others because they have lost the strength and the courage to face new situations. If we really value creativity we have to cultivate, in our educational and social institutions, a respect for it and a receptive attitude to the changes that it may bring. This does not mean an *acceptance* of every change that it may precipitate but a respect for creative minds, an openness of attitude and a readiness to assess and assimilate change if it is likely to be beneficial. A tame acceptance of what is right and a fear of the unknown are serious impediments in the way not only of man's progress but of his fulfilment and self-realization. His creative role in the world is defined perceptively in a small poem by Iqbal in which the voice of God addresses man in these words.

Art thou alive? Be eager, be creative.
Like Us, take the universe in thy grasp.
Shatter info bits what is uncongenial
And build a new world out of the depths of thy being,
The free man finds it irksome to live
In a world of others' fashioning.
He who has not the power to create
In nought but an agnostic and unbeliever in Our eyes.

A novel definition of the agnostic and unbeliever, in terms which are not narrowly religious but measure the worth of man in terms of his creativity.

Such creative mind is deeply and passionately involved in his work and finds true satisfaction and joy in it. His source of happiness is within himself; he does not depend for it passively on external stimuli and mass media which often tend to kill creativity. He may enjoy them occasionally as a diversion when they take the place of active creation, it lowers the whole quality of life. He then becomes increasingly incapable of facing solitude, of being with himself. Confucius is said to have remarked that most evils arise in the world because, man is afraid to be alone with himself in his own room'. T.S. Eliot stressed this point in his own way by saying 'Man is not himself unless he is a member (of society) and he cannot be a member unless he is also something more. His membership and solitude must be taken together. There are moments, perhaps not known to everyone, when a man may be nearly crushed by the terrible awareness of his isolation from every other human being and I pity him if he finds himself alone with himself and his meanness and futility alone without God'. A creative, individual must, therefore, keep his relationship alive both with society and solitude, finding his scope for service in the former and discovering his inner spiritual resources in the latter.

It has been man's tragedy, as well as challenge that while his promise and potentialities are limitless, his achievement so far has been far shorter of his goal—he holds, as it were, a goblet full to the brim in a palsied hand. The palsy may be physical or spiritual but it is the latter that is more dangerous. Man can achieve his destiny if he continues progressively not only to perfect his tools but also to refine and define his purposes more perceptively and more comprehensively. In the great progress that he has made in the last hundred years, the emphasis has been on the former, *not* on the latter. The power that has come to him in such ample measure through the conquest of the world of matter has been applied only in a modest measure to fight against the age-old deprivations from which men suffer and to achieve beneficent social aims and purposes which would humanize and dignify life. It has been used much more to increase material production or to perfect the instruments of self-destruction. Power by itself is a dangerous gift—whether it is political power or technological power—unless it is wedded to vision and dedicated to the improvement of the condition of man. It is really the illumination of the end which ennobles the means, though it is also true that unless the means adopted are pure, the purity of ends cannot be preserved. Man cannot realize his infinite promise and achieve his destiny, unless to his creativity and his social sensitiveness are given the best possible conditions for development. I repeat this 'destiny' is by no means a pre-determined destiny but a *possible* destiny. And the possible cannot be translated into the actual without persistent and dedicated effort and a resolute will to fight against the forces which pull him downwards and which are also to some extent, an integral part of his native equipment. The Semitic religions regard 'angels' as being *incapable* of wrong doing, but man is adjudged to be superior to them because he has been given the perilous freedom to do either right or wrong:

> We have shown him the path; he can now either accept it thankfully or deny it.

In other words, the right of free choice makes life's burden harder as well as more challenging. It is only through the gradual transformation and sublimation of his lower instincts and impulses—*not* their suppression and denial—that he can advance towards his ideal self. The modern tendency to emphasize the importance—as, for instance, by some psycho-analysts—of what I have ventured to call his 'lower self' is good if it does not result in our accepting is an inevitable or incurable but as a *fact* of life with which we must reckon. It is a protection against the easy optimism from which many good-intentioned persons suffer. It is bad, if it induces the belief that nothing can, and therefore need, be done about it, that it is an integral and permanent part of man as his 'higher self' and that man's business is only to try and *understand* human nature and 'to understand all is to forgive all'. I venture to suggest that man's adventurous journey throughout history has been in search of greater beauty, greater goodness, greater truth, greater creativity, greater justice and a better harmonization of these, both in individual and collective life. This is not to belittle the injustice, the cruelty, the exploitation of man by man that has characterized his historic development. It is really an attempt to see man in the right focus and to distinguish between what is of permanent value and what represents vestiges of long, unhappy past and a de-educative environment which, one hopes, may disappear in course of time. Jawaharlal Nehru summed up, in one of his speeches, his fine testament of faith:

> 'I see in this past the long struggle of Man against adverse surroundings. I see his repeated martyrdom and crucifixion but I also see the spirit of man rising again and again and triumphing over every adversity. We may be a speck of dust on a soap bubble universe but that speck of dust contained something that was the mind and spirit of man. More wonderful than the earth and heavens is this spirit of man which grows ever mightier and seeks fresh worlds to conquer.... Inspite of innumerable failings, man

throughout the ages has sacrificed his life and all he held dear for an ideal for truth, for faith, for country, for honour. That ideal may change but that capacity for self-sacrifice continues, and because of that much may be forgiven to man and it is impossible to lose hope for him. In the midst of disaster he has not lost his dignity or his faith in the values he cherished.'

He knows that the future is dark and uncertain and yet his optimism cannot be defeated. 'We can see part of the way leading to it and can tread it with firm steps, remembering that nothing that can happen is likely to overcome the spirit of man which has survived so many perils. Remembering also that life for all its ills has joys and beauty, and we can always wander, if we know how to, in the enchanted woods of nature.

What else is wisdom? What of man's endeavour
Or God's high grace, so lovely and so great?
To stand from fear set free to breathe and wait;
To hold a hand uplifted over Hate:
And shall not Loveliness be loved for ever?'

When this happens, when some objectives outside beyond and greater than the individual's own self challenge and capture his whole-hearted loyalty and imagination, when his life urges express themselves in many worthy and impersonal interests, man's small and isolated self becomes part of the great stream of life. The man ceases to feel timid or insignificant because he knows that something of his own will abide long after his own candle has gone out—in the good that he has done, in the creative thinking of the world which he has advanced or the contribution that he has made to art or literature or culture, intellect or beauty. Then this rivulet becomes part of science or other manifestation of the ocean, this mortal puts on the mantle of immortality and death ceases to have any terror for him. This is the concept of man which I venture hesitantly to place before you—of man the proud, the courageous, the compassionate, who will not lay down his arms before the cosmic forces of destruction and death but continue to light his candle though darkness may encompass the world; of man as mirrored in the stirring words of Russell.

> 'Brief and powerless is Man's life; on him and all his race the slow, sure doom falls pitiless and dark. Blind to good and evil, reckless of destruction, omnipotent matter rolls on its relentless way; for Man, condemned today to lose his dearest, tomorrow himself to pass through the gate of darkness, it remains only to cherish, are yet the blow falls, the lofty thoughts that ennoble his little day; disdaining the coward terrors of the slave of Fate, to worship at the shrine that his own hands have built; undismayed by the empire of chance, to preserve a mind free from the wanton tyranny that rules his outward life; proudly defiant of the irresistible forces that tolerate, for a moment, his knowledge and his condemnation, to sustain alone, a weary but unyielding Atlas, the world that his own ideals have fashioned despite the trampling march of unconscious power.'

8

Maulana Azad as I Knew Him

Maulana Azad as I knew him? What do I know of Maulana Azad? What does a man on the ship know of a gigantic iceberg of which he sees only a small portion jutting out of water? Or a person living at the bottom of a majestic mountain know of its snow capped peaks on which a perpetual peace *seems* to reign, of its winding rivers and valleys, of the storms that rage and the lightnings that flash round its head or the flaming lava that see these within its bosom? Or of its wealth of vegetation and trees and flowers and precious stones? No, it is only when we see it from a proper distance that its full impressiveness comes home to us. And we, of this generation, will not be able to appreciate fully the personality of Maulana Azad, cast in a titanic mould, till time has given us the correct perspective. I have a haunting sense of inadequacy, when I think of him or try to speak or write about him.

Maulana Azad as I knew him? I knew him, first and foremost, as a man of uncompromising integrity and high principles. In 1920, when I was a young student, I wrote to him asking what one should do at that critical time. Prompt came the reply in the form of a verse from the Quran:

> Cooperate with all that is good and virtuous and do not cooperate with anything that is evil and unjust.

I think this verse aptly sums up his basic declaration of faith. There are very few persons in our public life in whom, as someone has said, the gulf between precept and practice, between word and deed, was so tenuous as to be almost invisible. He was ever ready to cooperate with what he considered right, irrespective of affiliations of religion or caste or creed and he was equally adamant in withholding cooperation from everything that savoured or injustice or corruption, even if persons nearest to him were involved in it in anyway. Rightly has he been described as the 'conscience of the nation'

Maulana Azad as I knew him? I know him, in the words of Pandit Nehru, as a 'bridgo' between the cultures of the East and the West, as the man who magnificently spanned in his person the gulf between the past and the future. Every great culture develops its characteristic values, attitudes and ideals after a travail of centuries and, in the course of its history, it produces many good and great individuals. But, sometimes, it happens that, in a burst of creation, these values find an artistically perfect expression in a single human personality—in a Leonardo da Vinci, or a Goethe or a Arbaham Lincoln or a Tagore or a Gandhi or Nehru. In fact, it is a rare and remarkable phenomenon that India should produce *several* such personalities in the course of a single generation. Azad was cast in the same kind of mould and was an outstanding product of the gracious Indo-Semetic culture which had ripened during the last thousand years. But he was more than a mere summation of the best in the past—its courtesy, its tolerance, its mellowness, its feel for spiritual values, its striving for perfection, its sensitiveness to humanism. He also represented, in his person, a creative leap into the future, because he had assimilated into his inherited cultural riches some of the best values and attitudes from the West—its objectivity, its scientific spirit, its intellectual integrity, its sense of justice, its concern for the common man. To some extent, we of this generation and all products of this cultural interaction, but in no one that

I know has this fusion into an integrated pattern been so beautifully achieved as it was in Maulana Azad. Without any English education, without speaking or writing in English, he was as easily and effortlessly at home in Western culture as in Eastern or Islamic culture. Nothing that was good was a stranger to him.

Maulana Azad as I knew him? I knew him as a person whom Nature had gifted so lavishly that it left one with a sense of bewilderment. What did he not have? A physical personality that would make him stand out in any crowd—even in death, his face had a beautiful majesty of its own.... A mind that was 'luminous' (as Panditji put it, with his unerring instinct for the right word and the right idea)—that is, not only capable of giving light to others but illumined, as it were, by some inexhaustible source of light for within. I can endorse from personal experience the tribute that almost everyone has paid to his capacity for sizing up a situation, for appreciating the basic issues involved and for coming to clear-cut decisions. While, in dealing with complicated cases, we would struggle with details and hesitantly weigh pros and cons, his rapier-like mind would cut through the padding to the core.... A heart that was open as the skies and unruffled as the ocean. No room in it for any kind of narrowness—neither religious nor-communal, nor linguistic nor regional. Every minority group in the country had confidence in him; they knew that, with his tolerance, his humanism, his incorruptible sense of fair play, he will see to it that their reasonable rights are protected.... He was one of the greatest masters of the art of writing and speech in Urdu that this country has produced. Those who cannot read Urdu can have no idea of the power and magic and fire of his writings which, since the early decades of this century, intoxicated and enthralled his readers and shaped the pattern of thought and feeling in millions of youth. The only other Urdu writer that I can think of, who has the same forceful impact on the mind of his generation, was official conferences can have no inkling of his real oratorical ability which was a inspiration and a terror in the magnificent days of our war of freedom. I heard him for the first time in 1920 at Aligarh. For six long hours, till about two in the morning, he kept his audience spell-bound—not a single person stirred from his seat!... He had a range of knowledge and a gift of memory which made him a veritable encyclopaedia—except that an encyclopaedia is static and has no originality or vision to give new interpretations, while *his* mind was like lighthouse which would illumine with fresh meaning and subject to which it turned. In him science and philosophy, religion and politics found a remarkable synthesis. For him, all these activities, intellectual or practical, were valuable only if they could be focused on one master objective—the evaluation of the 'good life' both for the body and the spirit, for the individual and the community.

Maulana Azad as I knew him? I knew him as a man who lived the intense life of the thinker as fully and nobly as the intense life of the man of action. He threw himself into the epic of the national struggle, when it called for suffering and sacrifice and physical courage and firmness, and when freedom was achieved, he guided the nation, during its early years of storm and stress, with serene wisdom, moral courage and uncompromising integrity. In his last years, due to a variety of reasons, including his failing health, his life was rather like that of the lonely eagle. But it is a remarkable thing that this did not cut him off from the significant currents of national life but enabled him to see it steadily and see it whole, assessing its weaknesses and directing its development with clear sighted vision. In the words of Iqbal, he was:

Misle khurshid-e-sahar fikr ki tabani men
shama-e-mahfil ke tarah sab se juda, sab ke rafiq

Like the mornig sun in the luminosity of his intelligence,
Like the candle in the *mahfil,* which gives light to all but is aloof from all.

Maulana Azad as I knew him? I knew him as a man of enormous self-confidence and dignity who never courted popular favour but won his abiding place in the heart of his people on his own terms. And this man, who was a king amongst men and a perfectionist in all that he did, was also like *faqir* who had no house, no property, no bank balance, no external trappings of greatness, not even the ordinary social ties that make cowards of men. I have seen no other great man more indignantly averse the every kind of self-advertisement or propaganda. He would not allow any organization or association or institution to be named after him; he would not accept honorary Degrees from Universities; he would even conceal his date of birth lest his friends and admirers should celebrate it in some way! I would sometimes remonstrate with him when such requests were made to him, 'Maulana, these people are really sincere; that want the association of your name as a expression of their deep respect and admiration'. 'May be', he would reply, 'but I have made a principle of it; I do not want anyone of associated anything with my name so long as I am a Minister'.

Maulana Azad as I knew him? This patrician, this aristocrat in body and mind, had a deep respect and compassion for the common man. One saw it in the sympathy with which he dealt with their problems and his sensitiveness to their distress. Once he refused, with adamant determination and in the face of all kinds of pressure, a Congress ticket to a very wealthy and influential candidate who was reported to have done black marketing of foodgrains. 'I can forgive almost any other sin or crime: I cannot forgive profiteering from the distress of the common man'. Such things are know well enough to many people, but perhaps it might be a revelation to many to read in this context the moving Dedication of his 'Commentary on the Quran' to a poor, unknown stranger:

'In December 1918 I was interned at Ranchi. As I came out of the mosque after the evening prayer, I had the feeling that someone was following me. I turned round to find behind me a man wrapped in the blanket.

'Do you want to say something to me'?

'Yes, Sir. I have come from a long distance'.

'From beyond the frontier'.

When did you reach here'?

'This evening. I am a poor man. I walked from Kandhar to Quetta where some fellow countrymen—merchants—employed me as a servant and brought me to Agra. From Agra I have come here on foot.'

'They made you take all this trouble?'

'So that I may get from you some elucidations about the Quran. I have read every single word of Al-Hilal and Al-Balagh.'

This man stayed there for a few days (studying the Quran) and then left without intimation. He did not see me before his departure, lest I should give him money for his return journey'. He did not want to burden me. I am sure he must have *walked* most of the way back.

I do not remember his name. I do not even know whether he is dead or alive. If I had not forgotten his name, I would have dedicated this book to him.'

This dedication was written in 1931, thirteen years after the incident. Dedicating his magnum-opus—this Commentary on the Holy Quran —to a poor, anonymous commoner from another land is one of the finest and most gracious gestures of the kind that I know of.

Maulana Azad as I knew him? I cannot speak of him here as a source of my intellectual and spiritual inspiration or as my Minister, at whose feet it was my privilege to work for seven years and to learn some of the most valuable lessons that give meaning to life and quicken life in the world of meaning. That is a story which must wait—it cannot be compressed in a short paragraph. I can only say that the stamp which he has placed on our national education during the ten years of his stewardship will long endure and deepen in the decades to come. I may, however, recall here, with poignant interest, the content of the three speeches that he made in the last two weeks of his life. In the first speech at the Urdu Conference, he spoke feelingly of the opportunity that must be given to *all* languages to develop and enrich themselves, of the part that all should take in the development of Hindi, and of the claims of Urdu to be cherished as solicitously as any other national language. In the second speech at the Central Advisory Board of Education, he referred to his persistent efforts of secure for education the place that it deserves in national life and the resources which the Planning Commission must make available for this purpose. I have never seen this man of iron reticence so passionately moved or use such words as he did that day to plead the cause of education before the bar of public opinion. And in the third speech at the Indian Council for Cultural Relations, he spoke of India's yearning for peace and its ceaseless efforts to spread its message of love and friendship to all nations. It seems to me as if, in these three utterances, he was leaving for us his last will and testament.... How can we sum it up? Be just in your dealing with *all* your countrymen, for justice is the foundation of the 'good life'. Bring an attitude of love and friendship and understanding to bear on your international relations, for you can only evoke good in others if you are good to them. And let education have the pride of place in your scheme of things, for without sound education you can neither place individual life nor national life nor international relations on a sound moral basis. And that, as I have said, was the supreme object of all his efforts, whether in the domain of education or politics, and it formed the inspiration of his epoch-making work in the field of religion, philosophy, literature and other branches of knowledge.

Maulana Azad has ended his epoch journey. The glorious caravan of his life has come to its appointed end—an end which I found epitomized in the following verses which caught my eyes as I opened the Quran on the morning of his death:

> O thou, whom the Lord has blessed with the quality of peace,
> Return to the bosom of thy Maker!
> He is content with thee, as thou are content with Him!
> Come and join the company of my elect!
> Come and enter thy above in paradise.

9

A Great Indian Poet—Iqbal

It is a great pleasure and privilege for me to have this welcome opportunity of speaking to you about a great modern poet of India, Iqbal, for whom I have a very high admiration and who, I believe, is destined to rank amongst the greatest thinkers and poets of this country. My pleasure is, however, somewhat marred by the fact I cannot speak to you in your own beautiful and sweet language and, therefore, your patience may be somewhat tried by first hearing me in English and then listening to the French translation. My own French is so inadequate and my accent strikes my own ears as so unsatisfactory that I dared not accept the suggestion of Professor Meile to address you in French. However, I hope you will bear with me because it is all in a good cause—the cause of international understanding and appreciation. It has always struck me as a cultural tragedy of the greatest magnitude that we who live today in a *small* world—a world shrunk to a fraction of its size because of the development of the new and incredibly quick means of physical and intellectual communication—should be so ignorant about the great men of other nations and countries. Unfortunately, countries and peoples are generally known, not through their great men of science and culture or originality and vision, whom they have produced, but through their politicians, plutocrats, war makers and war mongers i.e. not through people who create and serve but people who destroy and exploit. Thus the whole world knows about an obscure and unsuccessful house painter called Adi Shicklegruber because he exploited and misled and poisoned the mind of the German nation and was responsible for an unparalleled measure of misery and destruction—the world knows him under the name of Adolf Hitler: but how many people here have even heard of the name of the great poet, Iqbal, about whom I propose to talk to you today—a poet who not only wrote poetry which was beautiful and lyrical and inspiring and dynamic but a poet who had a true vision of the dignity of man and his great destiny and who had a fine appreciation of the values and ideals which are necessary for the peaceful progress and spiritual salvation of mankind? There can be no true peace or security or culture or humanism in the world till we can radically revise our scheme of values and place first things first—creation above destruction, culture above conflict, cooperation above exploitation, quest for vision above the lust for power, the riches of the spirit above the treasures of the earth and poetry and science and music and art above the crude dreams of the nouveau riche—in a word Iqbal and Shakespeare and Renan and Plato above Hitler and Mussolini and Alexander and Olive and Dupleix. Of course, if you ask any one whom he places higher—Renan or Dupleix, Shakespeare or Clive, Iqbal or Chungez Khan?—he will give you the proper reply. But people continue to behave as if the latter were far more important than the former: UNESCO is, at least partly, an attempt to bring about this change in the attitude of the world and my speech today may be regarded as a slight contribution to this attempt.

II

Sir Mohammad Iqbal, who died a few years ago at a comparatively young age, was educated in India, and later took his Honours and Doctorate degrees in Philosophy from the Universities of Cambridge and Heidelberg, his doctorate thesis being on 'The Development of Metaphysical Poetry in Persia'.

He was also called to the Bar in London and, on his return

to India, he worked at first as a Professor of Philosophy for a few years and later began to practice as a barrister-at-law which he carried on, rather perfunctorily, till the end of his life. He was elected a member of the Punjab Legislative Assembly for one term and took part in practical politics for a few years, being once elected the President of the All India Muslim League. In recognition of his great services to literature and to philosophical thought he was knighted and was the recipient of several honorary doctorates. But all these tings were, so to speak, secondary and, to him, entirely unimportant. He was essentially a poet and a thinker and not interested in the least in money or honours or position or what people may think about him. Like all great and true artists, he was interested in his art and its repercussion on his fellow men and the impact of his philosophical thought on the mind of his generation. And it is an indication of his greatness that he was responsible, in a large measure, not only for moulding the ideas and tendencies of the intellectuals—particularly amongst the Muslims who understood the two languages in which he wrote—but even the forms and the symbols which they use now for the expression of these ideas. Amongst his important works are three collections of Urdu poems called 'The Call of the Caravan', 'The Wing of Gabriel', 'The Stroke of Moses' and six volumes in Persian—two long poems entitled 'The Secrets of the Self' (Which has been translated into English by Professor Nicholson of Cambridge), and 'The Mysteries of Selflessness', 'The Message of the East', 'Jawid Nama', 'Zahur-i-Ajam' and 'What should the Nations of the East do'. He also published in English a collection of his lectures on the problem of Religion in the modern world, under the little of 'Lectures on the Reconstruction of Religious Thought in Islam' through which, mainly, he is known to the English knowing orientalists. He had the great advantage of being educated thoroughly in oriental and Islamic learning as well as in the best that modern European Philosophy and thought have to offer. He knew Urdu, Persian, Arabic, English and German thoroughly and had also a working knowledge of several other ancient and modern languages. But his chief attainment was not linguistic proficiency—there are many lesser minds with a far wider and more profound grasp of languages; it was an intelligent and critical study of their literature and philosophy and the capacity to assimilate their best into his system of though. His brain was like the workshop of the legendary master of alchemy who could transmute other materials and metals into pure gold. His poetry and his philosophy are not, mind you, a mechanical combination of diverse elements borrowed from the East and the West but a coherent pattern dominated by his own individual and distinct central *motif*. That is why his message has an importance not merely for the East or the West, or the Muslim or the Indian but for the whole human race or, at least, for those who are interested in the great values of the human spirit. In presenting this message to you, I am handicapped by the sheer wealth of the material at my disposal. He has discussed all aspects of life and touched them at many points—intellectual, emotional and instructive. His poetry is not like that of most other poets, merely recording in words of beauty the emotional moods of the moment, but taken as a whole, it presents a certain balanced view and ideology of life. Now, I can present this subject to you in two ways—either by attempting to give you a resume of his philosophy of life which, I am afraid, will have to be too brief and sketchy and may not interest many of the audience or by selecting a few of his central ideas and presenting them to you briefly with quotations taken from his Urdu and Persian poetry. I propose to adopt the latter course, because it might make the appeal wider and because it would make economy of time possible. However, there is one warning that I must give at the outset. As you know, there is nothing more difficult in the world then to translate poetry from one language to another; all the wealth of associations and the rich literary content, all the allusions and the fascinating suggestiveness which belongs to the words used by a master of the language cannot possibly be captured in a translation. Often, the literal meanings are caught in the net while the spirit, the flavour, the aesthetic significance slips out. And the difficulty is, of course, greater when translation has to pass through several languages, as in this case, when I have had to translate from Urdu or Persian—which is *not* my mother tongue—into English (which, again, is not my language) and a kind friend has been good enough to render the English translation into French. So, if you fail to catch the poetic spark, the fault is partly mine and partly that of the situation as a whole, in which the spirit of one man cannot talk to that of another without making use of crude and halting symbols. Subject to these remarks, I hope I may be able to convey to you something of the rich significance of Iqbal's thought as well as the gracious and arresting style in which he has expressed it.

III

Let me introduce to you in the first place his conception of the role which literature and poetry, in fact *all* the arts, should play in life. Iqbal is not an 'escapist' in literatures; he does not believe that the artist should dwell in an 'ivory tower', cut off from the conflicts and tensions of every day life and devoted exclusively to the satisfaction of his aesthetic impulses. If art does not tap the deeper sources of life, if it does not enrich our appreciation, if it does not make our pulses beat more strongly, it is not lively and dynamic but dead. In their periods of decay, nations *have* produced such decadent literature an art which have poisoned the sources of their life:

The highest objective of Art is a yearning for the life eternal;
This fleeting breath, evanescent like a spark, has no meaning.
If it does not produce a tempest in the heart of the river,
Neither the mother-of-pearl nor the pearl has any meaning.
Nations do not rise in the world without miracles and if
Art lacks the vigour of Hoses' stroke, it has no meaning.

To the poets of the East his message is one of strenuous living and he calls upon them to give up their attitude of withdrawal and escapism and important whimperings against Fate:

> Hast thou the coin of poesy in thy purse?
> Rub it on the touchstone of life;
> For long hast thou relaxed on a bed of silk,
> Now accustom thyself to rough cotton;
> Throw thyself on the burning sands
> And plunge into the fountain of Zamzam;
> How long wilt thou lament like the nightingale
> And make thy nest in the gardens?
> O thou whose snare would do honour even to Phoenix
> Build thy nest on the high mountains,
> That thou mayst be fit for life's battle
> That thy body and soul may burn in life's fire!

IV

Now this attitude to Art is really a reflection of his attitude to life. Iqbal is the great exponent of the value and importance of *Individuality* which he calls *'Khudi'* in life. He believes that the highest endeavour of individual conduct and social institutions should be the deepening and the strengthening of *this* Individuality in *every* human being. As a humanist, sensitive to all the possibilities of growth and expansion open to the human spirit, he rejects the pseudo-mystic and pantheistic views which regards the Self or the Ego as a mere illusion of the mind, possessing no abiding reality of its own—as if the highest ideal of man is to lose his individual identity in the Absolute like the drop which slips into the ocean and ceases to exist as an individual entity. In his own picturesque words:

> The End of Ego's quest is not emancipation from the limitations of individuality; it is, on the other hand, a more precise definition of it.... Throughout the entire gamut of being runs the gradually rising note of egohood till it reaches its perfection in man.

He believed in the eventual triumph of the creative impulse in man which, according to your great philosopher, Bergson, includes 'the creation of the self by the self' like an artist painting a masterpiece.

Everything is preoccupied with self revelation,
Every atom straining to achieve perfection;
Without the passion for growth life is death,
In the achievement of Individuality lies approximation to Godhoad;
Through Individuality a grain of sand becomes a mountain,
If it is weakened, the mountain becomes a speck of dust;
Thou alone art real in the Universe
The rest is but a mirage!

V

Iqbal believes that Individuality can grow best in an atmosphere of freedom, which gives scope for self activity, and when the self can feed on, and draw its inspiration from one's own cultural heritage and achievements. The attitude of the mendicant, of Slavish imitation, of inferiority which the East had adopted in the latter half of the 19th Century towards the West, because it had gained great material riches and strength—is, according to Iqbal, a wrong and criminal attitude because it has weakened their individuality and make it impossible for them to contribute characteristically to the cultural and technical progress of the world. Cooperation certainly, but not 'sual' or asking or dependence on others: .

Asking disintegrates the Self
And deprives it of illumination
By asking poverty is made more abject
By begging the beggar is made poorer.

Again:

Asking disintegrates the Self

And deprives it of illumination
By asking poverty is made more abject
By begging the beggar is made poorer.

Again:

I did not borrow eyes from others
But preferred to look at the world with my own.

Through an effective presentation of this thesis, in a variety of beautiful form, he gave back to India and the nations of the East their self-respect which they were in danger of losing because of the dazzling affect of the material civilization of the West. He preached to them a gospel of active quest and striving which alone could give vitality to knowledge and wings to life. Here is an instructive conversation between a moth and a bookworm—the one burning for action, the other buried in the study of books—bringing out the superiority of active effort over inert knowledge:

I heard a moth in my library say to the bookworm:
Oft have I spent my time with the writings of *Sina* and *Farabi*
But I remain as ignorant as over of the secret of life—
Aptly answered the half burnt moth:
You will not find this secret in books.
For it is 'passion' which make life more dynamic
And gifts it with the capacity for flight.

VI

Iqbal does not, however, believe that knowledge alone can bring peace or salvation to mankind or provide a balm for the lacerated heart of humanity. In common with Bergson, he has raised his voice of protest against the over-intellectualism of modern thought. He wants to supplement the intellect with what he calls '*Ishq*' or Love and to the perception by the mind he wants to add the intuitive perception which is the distinctive function of the heart. Iqbal's great complaint is that the modern philosophic tendencies as well as the Socio-political situation have been so overwhelmed by the triumphant materialism of the age and the achievements of modern science that the values associated with Love, Intuition and the Religious Experience have been ignored, if not actively rejected. He is anxious to redress and restore the balance that has been upset by the civilization of modern Europe. Intellect, uninspired by Love and Science, uncontrolled by faith in ethical and religious values (which intellect alone cannot provide) have given Europe a ruthless economic system, an unjust social order, a bitter class conflict, a craze for armaments culminating in the most disastrous war in human history whose crowing climax was the Atom Bomb. All these things have made life full of strain and hurry and frustration and an incapacity for the quiet enjoyment of the fruits of leisure and culture. The modern man has really 'ceased to live soulfully i.e., from within and is living in open conflict not only with others but also with himself. He finds himself unable to control his ruthless energy and infinite gold hunger and power lust and these are gradually killing all higher striving in him and bringing him nothing but life weariness.' This is how Iqbal, visualizes with a haunting beauty of imagery, the dilemma of the modern man, equipped with Power but lacking in Vision, master of Means but uncertain and groping as to Ends.

> Love is non-existent and Intellect bites him like a serpent;
> He has failed to bring Intellect under the sway of vision,
> He, who has succeeded in tracing the stars in their courses,
> Has failed to pick his way in the world of his own ideas.
> He is so entangled in the mazes of his knowledge
> That he has failed to distinguish between Profit and Loss.
> He has ensnared the rays of the Sun for his purposes
> But failed to illumine the dark night of his Life.

He reverts to this theme over and over again in a hundred different, but fascinating forms:

> Whence does poetry gain its power? –

from the intoxicating lament of the heart!
Whence does this candle gain its light? –
from the fluttering of the moth of the heart!
What is this dark abode which they call the Universe? –
a worn out idol from the temple of the heart!

And:

When the Self is strengthened by the power of Love
It becomes the undisputed sovereign of the Universe.

Without the wedding of Intellect to Vision, of Science to Love and Charity, without an infinite respect for the human personality, which is the highest achievement of the Creative Evolution, we cannot possibly solve the *impassé* in which we find ourselves today and Iqbal had sounded this note of warning to the West decades ago, and it is only after his death that we have harvested the crop of wrath for the evil deeds that we had sown during the last few generations: Addressing the West he had said:

Your civilization will commit suicide with your own dagger;
If you build your nest on a delicate branch-how can you expect it to endure?

VII

But, if this fusion of Power with Vision can be brought about, infinite possibilities open out before the individual and Iqbal is a fervent believer in man's high destiny.

Let him explain in his own words how this infinite process of Creative Evolution is going on:

Think not that the tavern keeper's work is ended;
There are still thousands of untested wines in the vein of the vine!

Or:

Raise your Individuality to such a pitch of perfection
That God will consult you about your destiny: What is it that you desire?

If man is not original and creative, impatient of the old and outworn and anxious to launch on new adventures in the world of matter and the world of the spirit, then he cannot attain his high destiny and become a co-worker with God in implementing his purposes. Here is the voice of God appealing to man's innate creativity and freedom in the unforgettable words of the poet:

Art thou alive? Be eager be creative;
Like us take the Universe in thy grasp;
Shatter into pieces what is unsuitable
And build a new world out of the depths of thy being;
The free man finds it irksome to live
In a world of others fashioning;
He who does not possess the gift of creation
Is no better than the Agnostic and the unbeliever in our eyes.

This is surely and original and dynamic conception of faith and unfaith which lifts this controversy form the narrow regions of theology to the much higher plane of universal humanism, where art and science and culture and all that comes under the rich meaning of 'creation' find their proper place in the forefront of human activity. He is not afraid to challenge God Himself on behalf of Man, the creator:

You created the night I fashioned the lamp to light it.
You created earth, I made beautiful oups out of it.
You created deserts and mountains and arid plains,
I created beautiful orchards and groves and gardens.
It is I who have made glass out of stone!
It is I who have extracted elixir out of poison!

And he is often impatient of men as he sees them—inferior in mind, limited in vision, full of meanness and cruelty and greed—and raises his lament to God:

> Create another pattern, bring out a more perfect Adam
> It behaves not God, to fashion these playthings of clay!

And

> If the pattern is poor, what avails repetition?
> Art Thou satisfied with these cheap human specimens!

There is in this matter a certain similarity between his view and that of the German philosopher, Nietzsche who presented the concept of a Superman. But the *difference* between them is even more significant. While Nietzsche despairs of men as they are and is contemptuous of their powers and possibilities and hopes for the miraculous appearance of a Superman, Iqbal has faith in his fellow beings and in the power of right education and social ideology to transform them into better men and women by developing their inner wealth of intellectual and spiritual resources.

> The rise of Adam, born of clay, is a cause of alarm to the Stars,
> Lest this fallen star should develop into the full moon!

Thus Iqbal has 'an imperative vision of the divine in man' and he is anxious to use the agency of education to develop the Divine even in a plebian and thus open up before him an infinite future.'

VIII

I have already referred to the fact that Iqbal has greatly stressed the role of religion and spiritual values in life. According to him, the Iqbal and the Real are not two opposing forces and the affirmation of the spiritual self demands a willing acceptance of this world of matter so that it may become an ally and an instrument in our spiritual expansion and development. In his own words:

'The spirit finds its opportunity in the natural, the material and the secular. All that is secular is, therefore, sacred in the roots of its being. There is no such thing as a profane world. All this immensity of matter constitutes a scope for the self realization of the spirit. As the Holy Quran so beautifully puts it: 'The whole of this earth is a mosque'. So, he holds that it is only by flinging ourselves as good crusaders in the struggle for establishing the Kingdom on Earth that we can achieve the purpose of our life—not by shunning the struggle on earth because our head is in the clouds. To an enquiry made by his Indian disciple why, with all his knowledge and insight into religion, he has failed in the business of life, he cryptically replies:

He who can stride across the skies
Cannot find it difficult to tread on earth.

meaning thereby that anyone who is really gifted with the intellectual and creative activity of the spirit *must* make a good job of his life here and now. Otherwise all his pretensions to spirituality are false and unreal. From this you can also appreciate that his view of the role of Religion differs emphatically from the narrow clerical view which relegates it to a special corner in the mansion of life instead of visualising it as a dynamic inspiration for the whole of life. He puts these two views of Religion epigrammatically in the following words:

Religion is either a constant exalting of the name of the Lord in the vast expanses of the Heavens
Or night-long vigils of prayer in the lap of the Earth!
That is the religion of self-conscious, God-intoxicated men,
This is the religion of the priests, the plants and the stones!

So to Iqbal, the significance of religion lies in the fact that it is a dynamic force for heightening the tempo of life and the most powerful source of that idealism and love of humanity which alone can ensure that man will use his tremendous powers not for evil but for good.

> From the domain of Love, I am raising a new army,
> For in the holy temple, there is a danger of the revolt of the Reason.
> Think not that there is no accounting for the Intellect,
> The vision of the man of faith will weigh it in the final balance.

I shall in conclusion quote to you a few lines form here and there to give you an idea of how various issues impinged themselves on Iqbal's poetic consciousness.

Life of Struggle:

> Feast not on the shore, for there
> Softly breathes the tune of life;
> Grapple with the waves and dare;
> Immortality is strife.

Today and Tomorrow:

> Say not the world's work is crooked,
> For every moment of our life harbours eternity.
> Grasp Today firmly, for Tomorrow
> Is still in the womb of Time.

Despair not of man:

> Despair not of this handful of dust;
> Whose light is scattered and fitful;
> When Nature undertakes the creation of a form
> It brings it to completion in its good time.

The Light is within you

Looking for light, you went to Mount Taurus
For you are ignorant of your own self;
Go forth in quest of Adam;
God Himself is in that quest!

The Poet's Lament

What shall I do? My nature is not content with rest,
I have a heart impatient as the breeze in the poppy fields.
As soon as my eyes rest on a manifestation of beauty,
My heart begins to yearn for something more beautiful.
From the spark to the star, from the star to the sun—
I have no desire for a destination, for rest spells death.
With a restless vision and a hopeful heart.
I seek for the end of that which has to end;
The heart of the lover dies in an eternal paradise—
Without pain, without sympathy, without lament!

The Angels song addressed to God:

Intellect is still unbridled and Love homeless,
Eternal creator, thy creations are yet imperfect!
The saint and the sinner, the ruler and the jurist
Are all laying their snares for man;
The same old days and nights revolve in thy world!
The rich are intoxicated by their wealth,
the poor wrapped up in their misery—
The common man knocking about the streets,
the exploiter sung in his luxury.
Reason and Religion and science and Art are all enslaved
by greed;
For the grace of Love, unraveller of knots, is far from
being
common yet.
The essence of Life is Love, of Love Individuality

Alas that this well tempered steel is still encased in the scabbard!

And finally a few lines which are of interest because they throw light on the character and temperament of the poet himself:

The God-intoxicated *dervesh* is neither of the East, nor of the West—
I belong not to Delhi, nor to Ispahan nor to Samarkand!
I speak out that which I consider right—
Neither befooled by the mosque, nor a blind devotee of modern civilisation;
I have incurred the displeasure both of friends and strangers:
Why?—because I would not agree to dub poison as sugar!
Hard it is for one who sees and understands truth
To describe a mound of earth as the Damawand mountain.

This then is Iqbal whom I have the honour to present to you—a thinker of great vision and insight and intellectual integrity who understands the tragic crisis which faces mankind and a poet of great artistic ability and power who can transform his understanding, his sympathy and his righteous indignation into verses which are, in the words of the English poet, Keats 'a thing of beauty' and, therefore, 'a joy for ever'. If my talk can interest some of you in the study of his poetry and his thought, which is significant and possesses universal appeal, I shall consider that your valuable time and my attempt have not been wasted.

10

The Challenge of Badshah Khan

If I were asked to state what is the best thing that happened to India in 1969, I would unhesitatingly reply: The visit of Badshah Khan. In this age of power politics, of using unscrupulous means for not-such-worthy ends of life centering round the first person singular, one was almost beginning to forget that there *are* persons in the world even today who can rise above the self, and above the petty divisions and differences which cramp and cripple it. Persons to whom truth is dearer than power of wealth, who can courageously proclaim it unmindful of consequences, who are not only passionately devoted to the ideal of service, but in practising it, make no caste or creed or national distinctions. Badshah Khan came like a breath of fresh air in India—one could say like a gust of fresh air, if that expression can be used for a man, so gently, so soft spoken. I cannot say he swept all the cobwebs away but he did make some of us keenly aware that we were living, in a world and a country, swamped by unholy cobwebs. As many persons have said he has reminded us forcefully of Gandhi—he spoke the same bitter truths but with love and compassion in his heart; spoke them in the same soft inoffensive tone; refused to compromise in the social, political and moral criticism, but did so with a sincerity which was not only disarming but compelled every conscientious person to do some real soul searching. Criticism we have always had in plenty—people take delight in criticising persons belonging to *other* political parties, *other* ideologies, *other* religions, *other* castes, every one, in fact, except themselves which means their party, their co-religionists, their caste. But this is usually motivated criticism, partisan criticism. Here was a man who had come as a guest of the Government, to whom the Government and the people had done the highest honour—e.g. the Nehru Award, address to the joint session of the Parliament. It was open to Badshah Khan to receive these honours gratefully to make appropriate noises like visiting Heads of States, to compliment the Government and the people on their great achievements and then make a graceful exit. But then he would not be Badshah Khan, who during the freedom struggle, had won the hearts of his own people and of the whole of India, not by kow-towing to them, not by pondering in their weaknesses but on his own terms—by standing boldly for truth, for non-violence and justice, defying the power of the British empire, defying Pakistan, defying imprisonment, defying death when it stared him in the face. He was not likely, therefore, to bow down before the forces of evil, obscuration and fanaticism which had raised their head ominously in Gandhi's India. Like Gandhi, like Russell, he can stand, one man against the world, embodying in his magnificent personality the dignity of mankind, which refuses to bow down before evil, even as the light of a candle cannot be put out by all the darkness of the world.

I was present at the meeting when the Nehru Award was presented to him at the Teen Murthi House. I was also in the visitors gallery of the Parliament House when he addressed the members of the two Houses. I do not know how others responded to his speeches in the depth of their hearts—outwardly, of course, most of them seemed deeply impressed—but to me they were a profoundly moving spiritual experience so much so that, when he finished his speech in Parliament. I quietly walked out unable to talk to anyone. It was *not* that he said something quite new which no one had said, it was *not* that he is a great orator, with any unusual command over words. But the sincerity, the passion, the truth which lighted his speeches were irresistible—truth which derived its force from 'truthful living', which Guru Nanak has called more important than truth itself. It was the heart speaking to the heart using the simplest and fewest of words. He was *not* indicting the Government and the people like an outsider sitting in judgement on them from a high pedestal. He identified himself with them, he suffered with them, he spoke in the language of agony, he was 'a friend who had come to make them cry not an enemy who could after (hypocritically) make them laugh'. He had come to Gandhi's India to see what we had done during the last 22 years of freedom. Had we built up its economy, made it self-sufficient in food, improved the lot of the poor and the underprivileged, lighted any candles in their lonely huts, meted out even handed justice to all classes and communities? He is not a gullible person; You cannot fool him. He wanted to find out the truth. At the age of 80 years, he took the arduous risks of travelling all over India and see things with his own eyes. He was pained to find that we had become too much involved in the game of power politics, in looking after our own political survival and safeguarding our personal privilege and position. And 'we' meant not only the Government but all political parties and most persons, officials or non-officials, who wielded any influence or power. Few of us can take solace in the thought that our own escutcheon is clean. God, he seems to say, will weigh us in his implacable scale of justice and find us wanting!

And what is after all, his message? It is as old as the hills, as old as the oldest of the prophets and as fresh as morning dew. It is a message of truth, courageous, uncompromising, spoken firmly but in gentle words; it is a message of love and compassion, not to be mouthed as part of platform rhetoric, but expressed the idiom of service which knows no frontiers. A great Greek writer has written that every beautiful woman in the world is a friend and relation of mine. I do not know whether Badshah Khan will make that intriguing and aesthetic claim. But I have no doubt whatever that he can justly claim to be a friend of all men and women in the world who have had a raw deal in life, who have been victims of poverty or fanaticism or injustice or suffered persecution from any source. His clarion call, expressing steely truths in gentle words, challenges our conscience and goes like a rapier thrust to our heart. I wish I could say to the hearts of all of us, but, alas, there are hearts that nothing can move. There are persons of whom it has been said in the Holy Quran; 'Then your hearts hardened and became like stones or even worse, far from stones water has sometimes been seen gushing out and they have also been known to fall to pieces from fear of God.' But it is a challenge which every person with a conscience must accept in this 'moment of truth' which is also for us a moment for crucial decision: which way shall we move—towards justice, tolerance and compassion or towards cruelty, injustice, fanaticism, social insensitivity which are casting their grim shadow over our national life?

From what deep sources of his inner being does this 'gentle giant' derive his great strength? He has been able to conquer the self; he has no axe of his own to grind; he does not want anything from us—neither money, nor honours, nor even political support at the moment. He has come to give not to take—give of his love, his wisdom, his sense of justice. One prayerfully hopes that there are some of us whose hearts have been touched by the inspiration of truth as a result of our dialogue with him—touched not as a momentary quickening of our lost generosity but as the beginning of a spiritual revolution which, I would venture to say, is even more important than any economic or political revolution.

11

New Tasks before Jamia Millia Islamia

You have honoured me by inviting me here today for which I am deeply grateful to you but I am also very conscious of being unworthy of this honour, especially since only last year the Vice Chancellor himself undertook this onerous responsibility.

Your Vice-Chancellor is very dear friend and I respect him tremendously. I would be only too ready to serve him in every possible way but I feel most diffident to deliver this address after he has given his speech. Only a short while ago he had spoken on the subject of Religion and Society at the Institute of Advance Studies in Shimla and that address is still vividly preserved in my memory. He is playing a cruel joke on me by asking me to deliver this convocation address after he has spoken.

I have no choice except to comply with his orders but I cannot help asking this question, How should one respond to such a charming enemy?

If there be any justification for this request, I can only say that ever since the founding of the Jamia, I have been associated with this institution in some space or form. I have admired basic ideals for which it was set up the sacrifices that have been made in achieving those ideals the values enshrined therein the struggles and the suffering of its founders in experimenting and giving a new direction to education.

Whenever I think of the Jamia so many pictures flash across the mind, so many memories come back about half a mile away from Aligarh Muslim University, a few dedicated souls laid the foundations of this institution, setting aside the demands of practical wisdom, with no building and no assets, set into motion this labour of love (except for a certain restlessness of the mind and heart) they had nothing by way of basic infrastructure for an educational experiment. I would not like to name him, but the main organizer of this great experiment possessed little more than a certain restlessness of the mind and heart. Driven by noble ideals of self sacrifice and patriotic favour, he plunged into this enterprise invoking the help of the Almighty God and he managed to start this project with the help of sympathizers and to preserve in his efforts in spite of heavy odds keep it going.

The friends were many but I shall recount the names of a few. Maulana Mohd. Ali, who was the first Vice-Chancellor and Dr. M.A. Ansari and Hakim Ajmal Khan who shouldered the responsibility for the constructions of the building and identified themselves completed with its progress and well-being and Gandhiji who helped out in every crisis by giving moral and financial support by his love and encouragement to the educational philosophy enshrined in this institution.

From Aligarh, this caravan moved to Karol Bagh in Delhi. Karol Bagh lay in the outskirts and the efforts of Jamia were directed towards awakening a desire for education of a general awareness among the very poor and backward people of this area.

After some years, this caravan moved to Okhla, where there was plenty of open space and scenic beauty, but it was devoid of basis civic amenities as a result of neglect by the local authorities but this did not deter the founders who seemed to be altogether indifferent to the comforts of daily life.

On this occasion, one cannot help thinking to those good people who rendered yeoman service to this great institution but are no longer with us. Guerda Philips Bourne who forsook her own country and made Jamia her home forever. Shafiqur Rehman Kidwai, whose combined a very charming personality with a kind of selflessness. He had almost a childlike innocent expression and a total dedication to work.

Mr. Kellott who had a different life style and came from a totally religious and cultural background, yet he identified himself completely with the Jamia fraternity. Akhtar Hasan Faruqi served this institution selflessly and with total dedication for 40 years. He was a part and parcel of the Jamia community and there were many others like him.

Mr. Vice-Chancellor, if it was not somewhat improper to refer to an honourable guest who is present here today, I may be pardoned to talk about Dr. Zakir Husain who has lit many lamps in the course of his life. The brightest and lasting longest is the lamp of Jamia. We have always been convinced of this reality long before he had reached other heights, as becoming a Governor or the Vice President. In his endeavoring personality he enshrined many noble values of a high moral character and of a true Muslim. I would also like to mention the name of Dr. Abid Husain who served the Jamia with the utmost selfless devotion for thirty years. He enriched Urdu literature with his writings and the country with his enlightened and progressive thinking. And than there is Prof. Mohd. Mujeeb who has devoted a lifetime to Jamia turning his back to other profitable careers and has made a name of himself by writing books and giving speeches in English.

But why am I talking of this saga before people who have themselves contributed to its creation and nurtured it with their life blood. I am merely a commentator from outside who has seen this institution grow and develop. I merely wish to draw your attention to the fact that it is very necessary for every individual of every institution to remember and examine (evaluate) its past.

We should (take pride) feel proud (in) of our achievements and learn a lesson from our failures and examine our shortcomings. We should be able to offer constructive criticism and not blindly worship it, absorb whatever is good and help to throw out the bad. This is challenge before your and before the entire community. I am perfectly aware of the fact that we have a set of people in this country who condemn and regard as impure every and new idea, whether it comes from the west or the east I wish to discard it like a thorn. Such people worship the past just because it is the past. They believe that everything belonging to the past is pure and holy. The other group, which is comprised of scientists and technocrats, believes that the legacies of the past hamper growth. They are like chains that tie us down and prevent us from progress and advancement. My feeling is that both these groups are in the wrong. We cannot altogether discard the past, nor can we refuse to look forward. In the words of the Prophet of Islam, knowledge is wealth and it has no limits and it should be sought after everywhere, whether it is in the past, the present, nor the future. To cling helplessly to any one idea is against humanity.

Ever since the achievement of independence we have displayed a rare maturity of thought. I have not allowed our natural policies to be influenced by irrational thinking and narrow minded prejudices. This is because we have blessed by leaders like Mahatma Gandhi, Rabindranath Tagore, Jawaharlal Nehru and Maulana Abul Kalam Azad.

It is now the duty of our new leaders and thinkers and specially of our universities and colleges to instill the low mindedness and a progressive and national outlook in the citizens of this country and serve them from narrow minded and disruptive thinking. The new educated community should have a broad, humanistic outlook and belief in the universal brotherhood of mankind. We should forget our religious, linguistic and regional divides—forget that we are Hindus, Muslims, Sikhs and Christians, that we speak many languages Urdu, Hindi, Bengali, Gujarati, etc., that we belong to different regions, Uttar Pradesh, Punjab and Tamil Nadu etc. We should love our religion, our mother tongue and the region to which we belong but at the same time show respect to all religions, all languages and all regions. This world has many good and many bad things which belong to all of us. I should have the right to be proud of all the good things and be ashamed of the bad. The essential purpose of education is to erase the difference between self and the other, break down the walls that divide brothers and cut the chains the imprison our minds and hearts and when you hear the death knell, do not ask for whom the bells toll, it really tolls for you when this lamp lightens in your heart, it takes all humanity into its embrace—when Hazrat Ali was the Khalifa he had propounded that it was impossible for him to sleep peacefully at night if even one person had to sleep hungry in Madina. This sentiment has been expressed in these memorable words by a French writer 'No matter how tightly I myself shut my eyes, there must be some stray and hungry dog somewhere which will ruin my happiness.'

I have wandered off from the subject of my discourse, but I would just like to mention that this sentiment of compassion is not mere pity that is aroused in the heart of any man when he sees someone in pain or suffering and which is alleviated by giving some money to a beggar or shedding a few tears in sympathy—compassion, according to Gilbert Munay is a form of extreme revolt against an established and powerful authority against the entrenched customs, traditional taboos and the powers that be—It is the kingdom of God within us that revolts raises its voice against the tyranny of man. In this power-hungry and violence ridden world where personal gain and loss are the driving forces, there are people who work for the betterment of mankind. They give a meaning to life and are indifferent to personal gain.

Out universities have not addressed themselves yet to these moral and social concerns and if they do not do so, how will they create climate that can distinguish between right and wrong and true and false which will stand by truth and fight against falsehood which will guide society in the right direction.

If you give me permission, I would submit that the obligation is specially applicable to you since you represent Indian culture and civilization together with the Islamic tradition which had laid down that you must always speak the truth and stand by it even if it goes against your gain. If I remember correctly, your present Vice-Chancellor had conveyed this message to you almost thirty years ago.

> 'The Indian Muslims are as devoted to the land of their birth as anyone else. They are proud to be Indians. Their aim in life is to be good Muslims and good Indians. No Muslim can make them feel ashamed of being Indian and no Indian should point his finger at them for being Muslims.'

If is upto you to justify this statement and it is my fervent desire that this institution will always fight against lies and stand up for truth.

You, along with other universities, will have to maintain lofty standards and shining (lofty) values so that no one can even cast doubts on your sincerity of purpose or your intellectual integrity.

There will be certain disruptive and subversive organizations in the country that will try to lead you astray and oppose these noble ideals and the upholders of these lofty objectives. In a democratic society, everyone has the freedom to express their point of view. It is for you to stand on firm ground and not allow yourself to be swayed on misguided by such people.

The truth should be firmly entrenched in your heart and you should not allow yourself to be swayed by siren voices. There is no dearth of wicked people who will lead you astray. There are many Yazids in our midst, but very few Shabbirs—who are prepared to become martyrs for a cause. Life is a permanent battlefield, but people forget that wars are not always fought to defeat or harm an external foe. Gandhiji has taught us to fight the battle within to undergo hardships and suffering so that others may be served.

How can I forget that we have first fought an unholy war and we are trying to establish with great difficulty a temporary truce—We never wanted this war, but when it was inflicted on us we had to shoulder the burden. But war is a dangerous thing causing untold suffering, death and destruction and a colossal waste of money.

Pandit Nehru has written that war brings out the worst in humanity.

It is, however, true that war also brings out many patriotic and noble sentiments in man. We have witnessed during the last few weeks, scenes of national unity but basically, all decent human values are sacrificed in its course and truth is the largest casualty.

When I hear the radio from both sides, I cannot believe how decent human beings can become such bloodthirsty villains who pride themselves over the massive destruction of life and property.

I feel deeply pained by the fact that it was Pakistan, that started this war and they call it 'Jehad'. Thus giving a bad name to Islam. They preach hatred for India and Indians and call it patriotism. They ridicule Indian culture, which is composite culture of Hindus, Muslims, Sikhs and Christians and they were also a part of this very culture not so long ago. I wonder if these are the values being placed before university students and I fervently hope that they will not succumb these subversive trends and have the moral courage and the intellectual integrity of fight this vicious propaganda. They should proclaim that they will not allow the seeds of hatred to take root and barter away the innate feelings of humanity towards mankind.

We will not compete with our religious in propagating enmity and hatred towards one another. Our national leaders are setting a fine example in their public utterances and we should follow their noble example.

After years of sacrifice and privation we have a last reached a stage of fulfilment as a result of the generosity of the national government. I know that this is not any special favour granted to you, but you have only received what was your due. Others have already received these benefits, where as you have struggled for years before getting these facilities and I congratulate you on your success and it is my prayer that just as you have succeeded in facing all kinds of privations, you will be as successful in tackling (plenty) abundance, which in a way is more trying and difficult. Lack of basic means for survival, in spite of its physical discomforts poses a special kind of challenge and arouses sentiments of togetherness friendship and a sense satisfaction. It also builds self confidence and encourages innovative thinking.

When there is not financial stress, one tends to fall into a rut and a life of ease and comfort tends to make us forget the purpose and meaning of life and puts the mind to sleep. I sincerely hope that you will not tend to compete with others merely in the outward magnificence of buildings and the expensive equipments. This will be entirely against all your noble traditions. Jamia has always revered its teachers, and given them full autonomy and independence of thought. It has extracted hard work from them and made them feel that they are inextricable (fled up) associated with their students. It is no this very unusual basis that this unusual institution was founded and this was its main inspiration for a long time. Yu have to make a new constitution now and fervently hope that you will not forget that basic and unusual principle on which this institution was founded and you should also remember that to shoulder this onerous responsibility you require a broad vision and strong shoulders. You will gradually have to induct new staff who should be right thinking and in tune with your ideals and objections (be highly qualified themselves). The students of Jamia have been given special stamp of moral and religious education. Now they have to cultivate a quest for knowledge and to teachers have to develop an aptitude for research and make a distinguished place for themselves in the academic world.

The Jamia has to introduce new subjects in higher education and increase the number of professors in the existing disciplines. If there is only one professor in each department then there cannot be an exchange of ideas or a clash. Knowledge is growing at a very rapid pace. Different departments need to interact with one another. Interdisciplinary contacts of cooperation are essential for meaningful research. If every professor looks himself in an ivory tower there will be neither breadth of vision nor any depth and it will not be accepted in national or international aides.

I would like to say a few words on the subject of discipline. Every institution is a brotherhood of students and teachers is which they work together to acquire knowledge and to spread (disseminate) and increase the boundaries of knowledge. I do not regard them as two different entities: A mutually exclusive and antagonism.

I confess that I am a little old fashioned in this regard. I do not like students behaving like hooligans and aggressively and placing their demands before teachers and teachers dismissing them off-hand and then accepting them at the point of a gun. This is not what one regards as civilized behaviours.

The relationship between students and teachers should be one of love and respect. Both are engaged in the quest for knowledge, and in helping to mould the character. The teacher provides the light of learning because of his experience and the student his youthful exuberance and zest should be anxious to acquire that knowledge. In order to strength this mutually beneficial relationship one does not require material means but only the wrath of love and affection. In a good institution, the question of discipline should not ordinarily arise at all. But there may be some psychological problems with some students, which should be tackled with great tact by the teacher. Similarly some teachers and patience are also lacking a maturity and understanding that enables them to mould the personality of students. It is the duty of colleagues the handle such teachers with sympathy where there is affection and fellow feeling and patience, many difficulties can be overcome. It is sheer carelessness and impatience that makes mountains out of molehills. You have not encountered such ugly an unpleasant situation that have defaced other institutions of higher learning and I pray to God that you do not have to face them in the future also. But you have to remain vigilant all the time to prevent such incidents from taking place in your institution.

The students of Jamia who are passing out today after having completed their education, will be entering a world where life is changing and running at a fast pace, where hearts are broken and no one hears them. You will face new challenges in a world where there are unlimited opportunities and unlimited dangers. It is my prayer that in this difficult situation you will certain your probity, your humanity, your broadmindedness and intellectual honesty. All of you will not achieve greatness, but you can certainly be a good person. It is better to be good than to be great, especially if you have to adopt nefarious means to achieve greatness.

May God give you success in the examination of life and you enhance the name of your alma mater as you succeed in life's mission.

12

Aligarh Muslim University: A Retrospect and a Prospect

It is difficult, with the onset of old age to resist nostalgia and perhaps equally difficult to appreciate the changes that one has to live through in one's later years. And yet one often flatters oneself with the belief that one has been able to exercise more objectivity in judgement, inspite of the fact that there is no valid measure to compare subjective feelings. As I think of Aligarh, where I spent four years of my life as a student and about twelve years as a member of the faculty, I do experience a nostalgic feeling about the Aligarh of my days, as I have no doubt each generation of students has done to a greater or less degree. Every institution has its good and bad, strong and weak points and it is not quite reasonable to imagine that in 'our' time—whoever 'we' happen to be—everything was in fine shape and has deteriorated since. I have been reading recently the 'Ap biti' of Mir Wilyat Husain who was one of the first graduates of Aligarh and one of Sir Syed's earliest co-workers. A man of unsurpassed integrity and character, with an inexhaustible capacity for hard, dedicated work and a devotion to ideals which would appear incredible to most persons today. Even in his story of the first phase of Aligarh, written in his straightforward, unpolished language, one finds that there were many things which could be legitimately criticized. But the general approach of persons, closely involved in the new venture of faith, was one of idealism and urge for service and one could easily discern in them a genuine community of spirit and action. On account of the political climate of the time, he refrained from 'participating in politics', as the expression is understood today but they were undoubtedly committed to the idea of serving the interests of the community and the country, as they interpreted them.

When I joined Aligarh in 1919 two generations of our family—my grandfather and later my father and my uncle had received their education in the M.A.O. college and made their mark both in the institution and in national life. The impact that it made on me I shall describe in words which I take the liberty to quote from the convocation Address I was privileged to give at the University in 1962. 'I can still vividly recall how, over forty years ago, I came to Aligarh on a hot and stuffy afternoon in a curious state of hope, timidity and adventure, with a prayer not only in my heart but on my lips that I may not prove unworthy of the 'image' of this institution that I had learnt to cherish from my childhood. God alone knows whether that prayer has been answered and, in any case, it is not for me to judge. But I can assure you that that wish has been a consistent inspiration through a life of rather mediocre achievement. As I look back over this long stretch of years, I ask myself: what has Aligarh given me? And fond memory brings to mind a long procession of experiences, recollections, ideas and impressions, softened by time but many of them tinged with poignancy. It was here that, in the impressionable years of early youth, I sat at the feet of teachers—ranging all along the spectrum from the brilliant to the mediocre and the indifferent—and learnt to look at the world of men and things and the world of the mind with eyes of curiosity and wonder and occasionally of understanding. Within these portals, I learnt something of languages and the thrill of reading great books as well as writing and public speaking: something of history and economics and politics, and a little of science—just enough to appreciate its role in the panorama of life and to regret not knowing more. But it was not merely knowledge of many subjects that fell in the wayfarer's bowl but other gifts of great value—the joy of intellectual quest, a sense of companionship with many kindred minds and spirits which transcended differences of language, caste and creed, a love of books and a passport into the world of ideas. Out of these influences and impacts were built up gradually certain values, ideals and attitudes to which one learnt, at least, to pay lip homage and towards which one endeavoured to move in moments of intellectual and moral integrity. Life brought many pressures and temptations and disillusionments later. Yet I like to think that they could never quite wipe out the initial impulse to seek for 'the good life' in all its manifestations.

But this was not all. Aligarh not only brought me into vitalizing contact with knowledge and values and ideals but also with many persons of eminence and character in whom I saw the thrilling miracle of personality, of knowledge transformed into wisdom, and noble ideals and values brought to earth and mirrored in every day life. It was here that I first heard, in his dear broken Hindustani the clarion call of Gandhiji awakening the self respect of the nation: here that I first saw Maulana Azad, speaking in the University mosque till the early hours of the morning, in words of unforgettable power and beauty, repeating the age-old, ever-new lesson:

> 'Co-operate with all that is good and righteous, do not co-operate with evil and injustice.'

It was here that I participated in the great Jubilee debate in 1926 when the students of the University endorsed with great acclaim, a policy of united nationalism. It was here that I had the privilege of working with Sir Ross Masood and sensing the deep humanism which pulsated in that noble heart. It was here that I saw Dr. Zakir Husain shaping his mind and personality into a thing of beauty and—to take two quite different examples—Maulvi Tofail Ahmad, carrying on his quiet but determined crusade of social and national service, while hiding his heart of gold and his character of steel behind a modest and unpretentious exterior, and Syed Sajjad Hyder radiating warmth and affection and striking sparks of literary enthusiasm in those who came into contact with him. It was here that Iqbal came to deliver his famous lectures on the Reconstruction of Religious Thought in Islam and I had the good luck to see him at close quarters. It was here again that I had the first glimpse of that gracious and irresistible lady, Sarojini Naidu, who is and will ever remain an ornament to Indian womanhood, and the great Begum of Bhopal who was our first Chancellor. I have named at random a few of these sources of inspiration, because it is the duty of every one 'who has touched greatness' to share with the world the privilege which luck has brought him. There were numerous others—political leaders, high government dignitaries (who could seldom forget that they were dignitaries, Indians, foreigners, distinguished men and women in many different walks of life—who came in unbroken succession. Some of them left their deep impression on me, as they did on hundreds of others, making one feel that life was more meaningful than the skeptics and the dilettantes imagined! When I think of these and other truly great men and women of our generation—not men of specialized ability but persons of high intellectual and moral calibre, like Tagore and Aurobindo, C.R. Das and Moti Lal Nehru, Mohammad Ali and Maulana Mahmudul Hasan, Ansari and Ajmal Khan and Rajendra Prasad, Zakir Husain and Radhakrishnan—I ask myself where are their successors who will be able to fill their places worthily now or later? And echo answers in a melancholy voice 'where are they'.

'I have spoken to you, within the framework of personal reminiscences, of the many Arts and Sciences and skills which one learns in the University. They are all important but, permit me to remind you that the most important of them is the gracious Art of Living to which all other arts, sciences, skills and appreciations are really contributory. This we can learn best in a many-sided and balanced environment, where all that is good and great and gracious in man's heritage and aspirations finds its proper place, where no doors or windows opening on its fascinating vistas are looked, where all *Hikmat* (wisdom) is treated as 'the lost property of the Momin', to be welcomed with open arms, irrespective of the source from which it comes. For, true culture is the very antithesis of all forms of prejudice and narrowness which we must reject without reservation. And, just think how rich and varied are these educative resources which a University can provide! Science that gives power, Religion which brings vision, History that develops prospective, Literature which inculcates right attitudes and values. Technology which increases productivity and control, and the Arts which provide channels for self-expression and bring joy and beauty into life. Not only these, but different ages and religious have poured their characteristic riches into our cultural heritage—reverence for life which Hinduism has stressed, compassion that Christianity has preached, the concept of humanism and social justice that Islam honours and scrupulous non-violence and rejection of hatred for which Buddhism stands. In the past, when the world was divided into isolated fragments and neither men nor ideas could travel fast and freely, one could condone a certain insularity of outlook. But now, when the world has become one, when distance and time have vanished, when in the words of Arnold Toynbee addressed to the people of the west but equally applicable to those of the east:

> 'Our descendants are not going to be just westerners like ourselves. They are going to be the heirs of Confucius and Lao Tse as well as Socrates, Plato and Plotinus; heirs of Gautama Buddha, as well as Deutere-Isaiah and Jesus Christ; heirs of Zarathustra and Mohammad as well as Elijah and Elisha and Peter and Paul; heirs of Shanker and Ramanuja as well as Clement and Origen; heirs of Ibni Khalladun as well as Bousset and heirs of Gandhi and Lenin and Sun Yat Sen as well as Cromwell and George Washington and Mazzini.'

In the course of the last years of its life, Aligarh has sent out a large number of its alumini into national life who have made good as lawyers, civil servants, teachers, doctors, engineers, writers, poets, political leaders, patriots who fought against the foreign rule, some cowards and time-servers, too, who sided with it for their personal good. Amongst them are included men of excellence of mediocrity, of inferior calibre as is the case with other institutions, and many who may not have made any particular mark in public life but led simple, decent, God fearing lives of their own. In this way, they made their characteristic contribution to the good of the country and the community.

In my days, the College and later the University which came into being the year after I joined had not become so large as to be unwieldy. It provided for its members the warmth and security of close fellowship, and students, who lived and studied together for four years or more, often carried the friendships forged into their later life. For many of us this period provided one of our finest and most fruitful experiences. There were many things at Aligarh in which we took legitimate pride—its sportsmanship, its large-hearted tolerance, which as a rule, recognized no barriers in social relationships, its readiness to entertain new ideas and reluctance to close its mind to other ways of thought. This was at the time the general tendency, though there were occasionally forces which pulled the other way and things happened which made one feel uncomfortable. There was, for example, the policy followed by one of its well known Vice-Chancellor—to whom Aligarh also owes many other debts—who followed the policy of recruiting the faculty not primarily on the basis of merit and suitability or integrity of character but on influence and recommendation and whether the person selected was likely to become the member of his own clique. Often promotions and positions of authority and administrative responsibility distributed on the same 'principle': This enabled him to win in almost every issue which depended on voting strength. We resented this on principle, because he often used this strength to bolster Government policies and, even more, because it ran encounter to the basic *raison-d'etre* of the University.

But, inspite of occasional intrigues for personal influence and power, one had the feeling that their corrupting influence left a considerable section of the students untouched, that the relations between the staff and the students, amongst the students of the various communities and between the institutions and currents of national life were healthy. Politically, students, who were at all conscious, went different ways and this was as it should be. For, I do not favour the establishment of any monolithic approach in a University, which is apt to put blinkers on the minds of students. Inspite of these differences, there was in my days reasonable give-and-take and a spirit of mutual com-mendation which kept the dialogue going. When individuals and groups differed, it did not mean that they were not on speaking terms with one another, as is unfortunately the usual climate of opinion in our political and even academic life today. If a University, of all places, becomes a rigid, closed—in society, in which intellectual intercourse begins to stammer and other ideas and ideologies are not entertained at all, in which controversy is either taboo or tainted with bitterness, the very basic purpose of its existence is defeated. Students should be so educated that they are willing to listen patiently and with an open mind to all points of view, to express themselves with fairness and reason and not pledge themselves, without careful thinking, to any political or economic ideology. Always open to the humanizing thought that there is a conceivable possibility of their being in the wrong. Even if the bulk of students is pledged to any particular creed or ideology, it should be possible for the minority to exercise its right of dissent, provided it yields the same right to others. The tyranny of the majority and the minority in matter of thought is equally dangerous and reprehensible.

I have allowed myself to be diverted to this line of thought in order to stress the point that the present generation of students should examine itself and its line of thinking and conduct in this light. I am not sufficiently intimately in touch with them to be in a position to pass any judgement. But, from what I hear and read of students in general today, there seems to be a flight from reason and quality both in academic work and discipline. The fault is obviously not of the students community alone; all of us—teachers, educational authorities, parents and the adult community—are in the dock, too. High quality ot academic work has ceased to be a high priority with a majority of students—they are far too much pre-occupied with 'political' manoeuvrings, provoked by different parties and making 'demands' for their rights, forgetful of their academic and social obligations. The 'demands' my will be right but they are pressed in undesirable ways. So far as discipline is concerned, many students recognize no norms whatever and indulge in acts of uncivil behaviour, rowdyism and violence unworthy of any civilized individual. We came across this incidence of indiscipline in many other countries too, but they are often associated with demands which have some valid ideological causes having a global human or political significance. Protest against the war mongering policies of their Governments or racial prejudices or intolerable economic disparities or denial of freedom and justice to individuals and suppressed groups. One condemns the excesses and acts of violence committed as part of these movements but there is for them at least, the excuse that the objectives in view are laudable. The protesters have only failed to realize the mutual inter-dependence of means and ends—that, if the means are bad or impure or violent, they are unlikely to lead to good results. In our country, unfortunately, the ideological and unselfish motives are rare—it is often the selfish and unenlightened personal or class or communal motives which provides the dynamic for action.

This is the situation as I envisage it and it pains me profoundly, not only because of what is going on today but what are likely to be its consequences tomorrow and the day after. If the rot is not stopped *in* the Universities and *by* the Universities, where will it be arrested? If the salt loses its savour, as it is doing with alarming speed, wherewith will it be salted? This is a question which all of us—students, teachers, parents, Governments—have to answer at the bar of our conscience. I cannot answer it on their behalf—I can only do so on my behalf—for no *other* person's answer can become a genuine dynamic force in their conduct. I can only *raise* the question—it is you who must answer it—and answer it not merely with reference to the world of 1970's and its baffling and complicated problems but to the much more difficult problems which most of you will have to face in the 21st century, when by generation will have been reduced to dust. I wish only to draw your attention to this future—unknown, menacing, promising. This is not the occasion to attempt to draw its likely contours.

Biographical Sketch of Khwaja Ghulamus Saiyyadain

Khwaja Ghulamus Saiyyadain, who was born in 1904 in Panipat, Haryana, belonged to the family of Maulana Ataf Husain Hali, one of the main architects of the Muslim renaissance in the nineteenth century and a close associate of Mirza Ghalib and Sir Syed Ahmad Khan. Although Ghulamus Saiyyadain was still a child when Hali, his paternal grandfather passed away, it seems that even at this tender age he was able to unconsciously absorb much of the illuminations of the Islamic sensibility that represent the most powerful and beauteous aspects of the modern Muslim intellectual and literary tradition. Having received such a mental and attitudinal training, Ghulamus Saiyyadain was admitted in 1919 to M.A.O. College which soon became the Aligarh Muslim University, to do his graduation. At A.M.U., under the shadow of the legacy of the great intellectual giant, Sir Syed Ahmad Khan, he was introduced to an altogether different climate of ideas where the course of his mental training took a new turn. By now, he had already started spreading his wings and excelling himself in both speech and writing. His natural gifts of sharp intellect and ready wit weaved such a web of magic that both the teachers and students could not resist. Having done his graduation with flying colours, Saiyyadain found an opportunity to go to the University of Leeds, U.K. for higher studies in Education. He returned to the A.M.U. in 1925 to hold the post of Reader at the Teacher Training College. It was his initiation into a life of and in education. What started as a teaching assignment soon grew into a passion that thoroughly consumed him and became a mark of his achievement and identity. His total dedication and commitment to the cause of education and teaching resulted in his elevation to the post of the Principal, Teacher Training College, A.M.U., in 1930 when he was just 26. But even before this rise in status, he had already attracted attention of the prominent educationists in the country with his educational expertise being increasingly recognized. His reputation as an educationist was further strengthened when he was appointed to the committee on National Education, set up under the chairmanship of Dr. Zakir Husain, under the inspiration and guidance of Mahatma Gandhi. As a member of the Committee Saiyyadain made remarkable contributions to the finalization of the Wardha Scheme of Basic Education. It was the highest point of his educational accomplishments and from then on his life was solely devoted to the promotion of educational theory and practice in India and abroad. During the period, he served as head of educational administration and advisor in various Indian states. He retired from active service as Secretary, Ministry of Education, Government of India. Even after his superannuation, he was not spared and made to be associated with the educational planning and other activities in India and abroad. He was also regularly invited for lectures as visiting professor at various universities the world over.

Dr. Zakir Husain was second only to Maulana Hali in influencing and shaping Saiyyadain's thought and action. He had himself admitted time and again how much he owed to Dr. Zakir Husain for his development as an educationist and a civilizational activist. He came into contact with Dr. Zakir Husain during the preparation of the Wardha Scheme and gradually their relationship grew into a strong bond of friendship where Zakir Sahib was like an undeclared teacher.

This camaraderie was not only between two individuals but also a source of inspiration for many activities initiated for the promotion of education and moral values. Dr. Syed Abid Husain once wrote about this togetherness in these words:

> From here onwards a relationship between Zakir Sahib and Saiyyadain Sahib started taking shape to reinvigorate with thought and action the educational life of new India. The educational views of these two thinkers are yet to be studied and evaluated the way they deserve. When our educationists will concentrate on their views, it will usher a new era of educational thought where Zakir Sahib will have the place of the 'Father of Education' Socrates and Saiyyadain Sahib that of the 'First Teacher' Plato.
>
> (Editorial *Islam Aur Asr-e-Jadeed*, January 1972)

Saiyyadain Sahib had a very broad, all-inclusive and holistic view of education which encompassed all aspects of life of both the individual and the society as a whole. Education for him was not merely a vehicle for acquiring knowledge or information that provides means of livelihood but a means of shaping an enlightened human consciousness and complete personality which has a sense lofty human values flowing like blood in its veins. He says:

> As we carry on our teaching assignments from day to day, teaching lessons, correcting exercises, supervising projects and experimental work, organizing games and social activities, we should be constantly asking ourselves many basic questions and taking the risk of giving honest replies: 'Are we quickening our students' minds? Are we developing their critical capacities which will turn mercilessly upon themselves but sympathetically on others? Are we enlarging their sympathies and deepening their human understanding so that they will not think and feel and act in their narrow and dark grooves of class and creed and caste loyalties but in the daylight of national

and human interests? Are we teaching them to be honest and courageous and free in their everyday dealings or implanting unlovely complexes for which they will have to suffer and pay in the long run? Can they distinguish between the beautiful and the ugly or does their education leave them aesthically blind? Have they cultivated the humble decencies of civic life which makes for harmony and cleanliness and pleasant social relations or do they continue to act in uncouth and boorish ways when they are given their head'? I dare say that these things are easy to achieve but I am firmly convinced that they are the only things really worth striving for. They alone provide the touchstone on which you can test the genuineness of the coin that you are passing on to them.

(Jha Memorial Lecture)

Mahatma Gandhi's life and views had very thoroughly impacted Saiyyadain Sahib's heart and mind. To him, Gandhiji was an epitome of the greatness of being human and civilized in the face of the forces of barbarism and violence unleashed during the twentieth century. He considered Gandhiji a one-man army of human values armed with spiritual awakening and non-violence combating the mighty forces of dehumanization. What impressed Saiyyadain Sahib the most was Gandhiji's holistic vision of life and his insistence on synthesizing the material and spiritual aspects of the human existence. Saiyyadain Sahib's educational views can be said to be an effort to translate into practice many of Gandhiji's views on education, although they were undoubtedly very firmly rooted in his own creative genius.

Saiyyadain was a firm believer in Islam and was a practicing Muslim but his vision of Islam transcended the narrow interpretations and practices that have been foisted on this great religion during the course of history. To him, Islam represented a tremendous human and civilizing force that had played a great emancipatory role during the medieval age in freeing human beings from the bondages of fanaticism, bigotry and religious exclusivism. Saiyyadain Sahib viewed Islam as a unifying universalist faith that through its insistence on the oneness of God calls for the essential oneness and togetherness of mankind. Large-hearted tolerance and peaceful co-existence were the two cardinal principles that Saiyyadain Sahib viewed as the fundamental building blocks Islam provided for raising a truly peaceful and pluralist social environment where all human beings of all creeds, colours, languages and races can live together without any friction and contributing to each other's growth as human beings.

Index